UML Explained

UML Explained

Kendall Scott

ADDISON–WESLEY

Boston • San Francisco • New York • Toronto • Montreal
London • Munich • Paris • Madrid
Capetown • Sydney • Tokyo • Singapore • Mexico City

For more information, please contact:
Pearson Education Corporate Sales Division
201 W. 103rd Street
Indianapolis, IN 46290
(800) 428-5331
corpsales@pearsoned.com

Library of Congress Cataloging-in-Publication Data
Scott, Kendall, 1960-
      UML explained / Kendall Scott.
        p.cm.
      Includes index.
      ISBN 0-201-72182-1
        1. Object-oriented methods. 2. UML (Computer science) I. Title.

QA76.9.O35 S26 2001
005.1'17--dc21
                                          00-068990

G. Booch, OBJECT-ORIENTED ANALYSIS AND DESIGN WITH APPLICATIONS, (figure 10-6 from page 402 of the above title). ©1994 Benjamin Cummings Publishing Company Inc. Reprinted with permission.

ISBN: 0-201-72182-1

Text printed on recycled and acid-free paper.
ISBN 0201721821
2 3 4 5 6 7 CRS 04 03 02 01
2nd Printing   September 2001

Contents

Figures

Preface

When I started seriously considering writing a proposal for a book about the Unified Modeling Language (UML), Amazon.com listed about 62 books whose titles contained "UML." By my reckoning, 61 of those books were aimed at programmers and other highly technically oriented people. The other one introduced its example system more than halfway through the book and, a few pages into that chapter, started showing figures with *way* too many things in them for a beginner to be able to handle. It became clear to me that what was missing was a book that approaches the UML from the standpoint of what relatively nontechnical people need to understand in doing their jobs—like how to capture requirements—rather than starting with the diagrams, as most of these other UML books do.

I wrote this book literally for "the rest of us," people who see the UML from the outside looking in. *UML Distilled* (Fowler and Scott, Addison-Wesley, 1997), for instance, made certain assumptions about its readers, namely, that they were comfortable with object-oriented terminology and concepts and that, for the most part, they were already using one or another of the approaches designed by the "three amigos," the creators of the UML—Grady Booch, Jim Rumbaugh, and Ivar Jacobson. For every set of modelers and analysts and developers who sank their teeth into Martin Fowler's brilliantly conceived book, though, there were at least a few people who wanted to know about this cool language but didn't quite know where to start. If you're in that latter group, this book may be for you.

I'm not assuming any knowledge of object orientation (OO). (Note that although the UML certainly is applicable in non-OO contexts, such as data modeling, the language was explicitly designed for use with OO.) If you find yourself reading a definition you're already familiar with, you should be able to skip that paragraph (or subsection or section) without any problem. I've also focused on capturing what I think are the most important aspects of the UML for people who probably aren't at the center of development efforts but still need to know what's what. The UML is a pretty big language; I suggest you visit my UML Dictionary (http://usecasedriven.com/UML.htm) and the UML Resource Center (http://www.rational.com/UML) if you want to explore it in depth.

I made my living as a technical writer for 16 years, translating complicated subject matter into reader-friendly documents and manuals. Now I make my living as a trainer and mentor, teaching people about the UML and about the approach to software development that *Use Case Driven Modeling with UML* (Rosenberg and Scott, Addison-Wesley, 1999) advocates. I'd like to think that this book reflects my years of experience.

Organization of This Book

Chapter 1, Why the UML?, describes why it's important to learn about the UML. This includes an explanation of the crucial nature of visual modeling. The chapter also offers some history about how the UML evolved and an overview of the key underlying principles of the language.

Chapter 2, The UML and Process, explains that even though the UML is technically process independent, it's been explicitly designed to work within the context of an iterative and incremental process. This discussion includes an overview of the Unified Process and a look at how the phrases "use case driven," "architecture-centric," and "iterative and incremental" will appear, in one form or another, throughout the rest of the book.

Chapter 3, Identifying Relevant Real-World Things, describes how a project team uses the UML in identifying, and beginning to refine, the things and concepts in the real world of relevance to the problem that the team is trying to solve with the new system. This chapter introduces The Internet Bookstore, a proposed online bookstore that will serve as a running example throughout the rest of the book.

Chapter 4, Capturing Requirements, describes how people can use what are known as "use cases," which are scenarios that include user actions and system responses, to explore, negotiate, and refine functional requirements. The chapter also addresses the role that prototyping plays in the development and refinement of use cases.

Chapter 5, Expressing How Things Work Together, describes how a project team explores how objects work together to address the behavior specified by use cases, as well as other required system behavior. This includes a discussion of robustness analysis, which uses extensions to the UML that are specific to the Unified Process.

Chapter 6, Refining the Structure of Things, describes the tasks involved in refining and expanding the domain model, which contains the real-world things and concepts first discussed in Chapter 3, and how this effort happens in response to the work involved in modeling interactions (discussed in Chapter 5).

Chapter 7, Describing Flows, describes how you can use the UML to describe business and process workflows. The chapter also discusses how you capture the behavior of a system that can have multiple activities occurring at once.

Chapter 8, Tracking the Lives of Things, describes how the UML represents the lifetimes of objects as they carry out the work of the system. This discussion includes a look at how certain kinds of objects can exist in more than one state at the same time.

Chapter 9, Showing How Groups of Things Work Together, describes how a team can use various UML constructs and diagrams to illustrate how groups of things will work together in the system, on a conceptual level. This includes the UML definitions of terms such as "pattern" and "framework" that are increasingly important in the realm of software development.

Chapter 10, Describing How Things Will Be Built, describes the ways that one shows how the system being designed will actually be built, in terms of packages of software called "components," and how those components will be geographically distributed in the new system.

The book also includes a glossary, which contains definitions for all the terms introduced in the body of the text, and a complete index.

Background

This book has been in the works for a long time.

The story starts in the spring of 1996. I was living in Dallas, getting a little bored making my living as a technical writer, cranking out software documentation for programmers I'd never meet. I decided to approach Rational about getting some kind of job that would get me closer to actual customers.

That conversation didn't lead to anything in the way of a job, but it did lead to me getting a copy of the 0.8 version of the documentation set for what was then called the Unified Method, written by Grady Booch (who I'd heard of) and James Rumbaugh (who I hadn't). After a quick glance at the densely packaged paragraphs and the scary diagrams (one had 15 boxes and 19 lines), I put it aside.

My relentlessly curious nature caused me to pick up the book again soon after that. Then I spent several hours trying to make sense out of it. I finally realized that I was looking at something fairly significant, and that the only way I'd be able to really understand it would be to rewrite it. I was just beginning to follow the comp.object newsgroup on the Internet, so I decided, on a lark, to post a query that read something like this: "What would you think if a professional writer rewrote this material?"

Grady Booch wrote back and said "Go for it!"

This was more than a little disorienting. On the one hand, I was encouraged to get a positive response; on the other hand, I thought, "Great. The first thing I did is annoy Grady Booch." When I asked him what he meant, though, he told me that he and Jim and Ivar Jacobson (whose name would appear on the cover of the next version of the Unified Method documentation) were all likely to write 600-page books, and there was a good chance they wouldn't be ready for a long time. Then he said that if I were to write a concise guide to the Unified Method—say, 150 pages—people would buy it.

So, I put together a proposal and sent it to Addison-Wesley, on my birthday (never mind which one). I was pretty dubious about it, given that I knew almost nothing about object orientation, but I figured I had nothing to lose.

Over the next six months, the proposal didn't get accepted, but it wasn't exactly rejected either. I decided to move to San Francisco at the end of 1996, and soon after that, interesting things started happening.

I met the editor to whom I'd submitted the proposal, Carter Shanklin, at Rational's user conference early in 1997. He said that my proposed book wasn't going to be viable, but also that he was ready to do a deal for the first book about what was now called the Unified Modeling Language (UML), and that he'd be interested in having me involved in some way.

Around that time, I met Jim and Ivar. (Grady was at Oracle, so unfortunately I didn't get a chance to meet him then and thank him for helping me get to that point. Oddly enough, I was working for Oracle at the time.) There were various ideas bouncing around about how this book was going to get done, but in the end, Booch, Jacobson, and Rumbaugh weren't directly involved in the production of the book. Instead, Carter brought Martin Fowler, whose recently published *Analysis Patterns* was already getting great reviews, and myself together to see if the chemistry was right for cranking a book out in, oh, four months.

I had no idea whether we could come anywhere near meeting that deadline, but I figured I'd give it a shot. Martin already had about half the book written when we got started, which helped considerably. The first thing I did was take a chunk of about 75 pages of text and diagrams and turn it into a reviewable piece of material, making decisions about subsections and mixing up paragraph lengths and many other things—over a period of three days, which included one full day of work for Oracle—and we were off to the races. I guess *UML Distilled* came out pretty well, all things considered.

After the book came out, I wanted to publish something in my own voice, so I put together the first version of my UML Dictionary. This was based on the official documentation that Rational submitted to the Object Management Group (OMG) in the spring of 1997, when it was first seeking approval of the UML as a standard. The text was still fairly stiff, but at least I was getting a good handle on the material.

The Dictionary led to another book deal (*Use Case Driven Object Modeling*, with Doug Rosenberg), and now, here I am with my first solo book.

Acknowledgments

I'd like to thank the Academy...

Let's start again.

I'd like to thank the several thousand people who've played crucial roles in my development as an author. In alphabetical order...

Maybe not.

I'd like to extend special thanks to the following Lucky 13: Guy and Nancy Scott, who had the good sense to put me on the right path and then (mostly) stay out of the way; Jonathan Leach, intellectual foil supreme; Lisa Silipigni, who helps me remember every day to fight the good fight; Grady Booch, without whom I wouldn't have been able to write this book; Martin Fowler, for letting me produce the world's best UML book; Carter Shanklin, Paul Becker, and Ross Venables, past and present representatives of a class organization, Addison-Wesley; Doug Rosenberg, who supplied the inspiration for the running example, taught me how to do robustness analysis, and provides me a healthy living as a UML trainer and mentor; Laura Danoff, for at least trying to read my other books; Robert Pirsig, who posed the questions that keep me going; and Hunter Faires, the greatest teacher ever.

Kendall Scott
Harrison, Tennessee
February 2001
kendall@usecasedriven.com
http://usecasedriven.com

Chapter 1

Why the UML?

Let's start off by looking at why you should learn about the Unified Modeling Language (UML).

Why Model Software?

Software just isn't getting any easier to develop, despite the best efforts of computer language inventors, tool developers, and process gurus. Even relatively small systems tend to have large amounts of complexity. This is what leads people to develop **models**, which are simplifications of reality that help them understand the complexity inherent in software.

Of course, a wide variety of models have been in use within various engineering disciplines for a long time. Aerospace engineers rely heavily on models that describe the forces acting on an airplane; electrical engineers use very large models in designing telephone switching systems; civil engineers would be lost without their blueprints. Models taking other forms, such as the simulations used in high finance and the storyboarding that Hollywood directors use, also play very important roles.

The UML has been designed to help the participants in software development efforts build models that will enable the team to visualize the system, specify the structure and behavior of that system, construct the system, and document the decisions made along the way.

Visualization

Models help a software development project team visualize the system they need to build that will satisfy the various requirements imposed by the project's stakeholders. The aphorism "A picture is worth a thousand words" holds especially true when it comes to the work involved in developing software: much of what's interesting about a given system lends itself to visual modeling better than plain text does.

The UML is specifically designed to facilitate communication among the participants in a project. Some aspects of the language are focused on the communication involving customers and developers; others, on that among system architects and database designers; still others, on that among developers working on different pieces of the system. By offering a set of well-defined diagrams, and precise notation to use on those diagrams, the UML gives everyone on the team the ability to understand what's going on with the system at any point in time with minimal risk of misinterpretation.

Specification

To specify a model, in UML terms, means to build it so that it's precise, unambiguous, and complete. Various aspects of the UML address the specification of the many decisions that have to be made as a system evolves.

- Models built early in the project help focus the thought processes of the stakeholders and enable them to explore their options with little risk and at relatively little cost.

- As work proceeds, the initial models get fleshed out as knowledge increases and a greater degree of precision is required. These intermediate models focus on the key concepts of the system and the mechanisms by which those concepts will be embodied.

- UML models with large amounts of detail generally serve as fairly complete descriptions of the most important features of the final system. If the modeling efforts have been rigorous, viewers will be able to trace the elements of the later-stage models to their initial incarnations in the rough sketches.

- UML models can also be constructed from an existing system to assist people in their efforts to maintain and extend the system's functionality.

Construction

Of course, the ultimate goal of a development project is working code. A healthy number of the UML's constructs have direct or indirect relationships with constructs offered by the most popular programming languages, including C++ and Java; other UML elements lend themselves nicely to tasks such as physical database modeling and network layout.

A technique called **forward engineering** involves generating code from models. Visual modeling tools such as Rational Rose make it easy to get code started from UML models. **Reverse engineering**, the construction (or reconstruction) of models from code, can also be very useful. Ideally, a project team will practice **round-trip engineering**, which encompasses both forward engineering and reverse engineering with the goal of keeping models and code in synch to maximum effect.

Documentation

The combination of UML models and the other kinds of work products that come out of a development effort generally forms a solid set of project documentation. For instance, a complete set of use cases (see Chapter 4) can serve as a strong foundation for user guides and related training materials, and the realizations of those use cases, as described in Chapter 5, lend themselves nicely to use by quality assurance people performing white-box testing.

In addition to helping people who weren't involved understand the thought processes underlying the development project, properly produced models and related documents will often be reusable, in part or wholesale, in the context of other projects.

What Makes a Good Software Model?

At the heart of the philosophy that underlies the UML are a set of qualities that, taken together, identify a model as useful and valuable.

- *A good model suits the plan of attack that the team takes toward solving part or all of the problem at hand.* A model that captures essential abstractions and ignores nonessential ones is likely to go a long way toward offering a high degree of enlightenment.

- *A good model allows different viewers to see different levels of detail at different times.* The stakeholders of a project come at a system being developed from varying viewpoints; a good model lends itself to inspection at levels ranging from the executive summary to the gritty low-level details.

- *A good model is connected to reality.* Rigorous development and continuous improvement of a model are likely to result in behavior that closely resembles what the team can expect to see when the real system is unveiled.

- *A good model works well with other models in capturing all of the essential elements of the system.* As discussed later in this chapter, and also in Chapter 2, the UML encourages the creation of several kinds of models that are, for the most part, independent, yet offer ample opportunities to trace the likes of data flows and control flows.

Where Did the UML Come From?

Around 1989, a healthy number of different ways to do object-oriented modeling were making their presence felt. The next several years were a period that's now generally referred to as the "methodology wars," or just "method wars." When the smoke cleared, in the mid-1990s, three of the contestants were seen by most of the object-oriented community as standing head and shoulders above the rest. Their names: Grady Booch, Jim Rumbaugh, and Ivar Jacobson.

Ivar Jacobson's Objectory process came at a system first and foremost from the standpoint of users and the ongoing evolution of their requirements (see Figure 1-1).

Figure 1-1: Jacobson's View of System Development

Jacobson's *Object-Oriented Software Engineering* (Addison-Wesley, 1992) introduced the OOSE method as a simplified version of Objectory, which he and a number of colleagues developed while building large telecommunications systems for Ericsson in Sweden.

The "white book," as it's commonly referred to, contained the first full-length description of use cases, which immediately became widely used and which now sits at the heart of the UML. Objectory, as expressed in terms of OOSE, also serves as the foundation for the Unified Process, which we'll look at in the next chapter.

Jim Rumbaugh's Object Modeling Technique (OMT) evolved out of extensive work with data-intensive systems, and thus was strongest in the area of modeling the problem space. Figure 1-2 shows the key elements of the first step of the OMT methodology, analysis.

Rumbaugh's *Object-Oriented Modeling and Design* (Prentice Hall, 1991) described, in great detail, how to build three separate models of a system—one each for the static structure, the control structure, and the computation structure—in order to understand the problem before implementing a solution. Much of the notation we'll look at in Chapters 3 and 6 evolved directly from the original OMT notation, and many people around the world still regard the material about mapping the object model (which captures the static structure) to relational databases as definitive nearly a decade after its appearance.

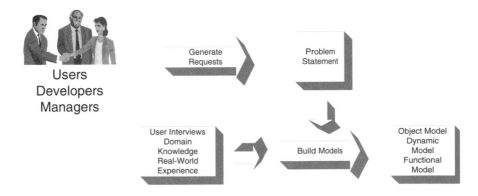

Figure 1-2: Rumbaugh's Elements of Analysis

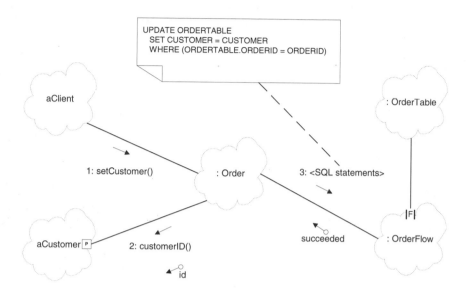

Figure 1-3: Booch's Detailed Design

The strengths of the Booch method (yes, that was the "official" name) were connected with detailed design and coding. Figure 1-3, which models a Structured Query Language (SQL) transaction, is representative.

Grady Booch's *Object-Oriented Design with Applications* (subsequently retitled *Object-Oriented Analysis and Design with Applications* [Addison-Wesley, 1994]) became a widely used college textbook. Its combination of rigorous attention to the details associated with building software systems and musings about architecture, philosophy, and cognitive science established Booch as perhaps *the* most influential figure in the object-oriented community.

The three approaches had enough common ground that mixing and matching became inevitable.

The initial seed of the Unified Method came in late 1994, when Rumbaugh left General Electric to join Booch at Rational. The company made the first version of the method public a year later, not long before Rational bought Jacobson's company and brought him into the fold. There followed the 0.9 Unified Method documentation, and then version 1.0 of the Unified Modeling Language.

Version 1.0 was what Rational submitted to the Object Management Group (OMG), the body that serves to define standards across many areas of computer science. After some negotiating with the OMG and the most prominent competitors in the race to standardization, UML 1.1 became the standard object-oriented modeling language in November of 1997. After a brief interlude during which a 1.2 version was in place, the OMG released version 1.3 of the UML, which is the version this book addresses.

Views of a System

The **architecture** of a system is the fundamental organization of the system as a whole. A system's architecture has a number of aspects, including static elements, dynamic elements, how those elements work together, and the overall architectural style that guides the organization of the system. Architecture also addresses issues such as performance, scalability, reuse, and economic and technological constraints.

Each of the various stakeholders in a software development project comes to the table with a different agenda. In turn, each stakeholder looks at the system from a different angle, and those angles are likely to change as the system evolves. The UML captures these angles as a set of five interlocking **views**. Each view reveals a particular set of aspects of the system from a given perspective, and hides, in effect, other aspects that are not of concern to the viewer. Figure 1-4 shows the five views of a system's architecture that the UML defines.

The **use case view** focuses on the scenarios executed by human users and also external systems. The contents of this view express what the new system will do without specifying how it will do those things. The next chapter takes a closer look at how this view influences the other views. Chapter 4 describes the key elements of the use case view.

The **design view** focuses on the things that form the vocabulary of the problem that the system is trying to solve and the elements of the solution to that problem. This view encompasses both static, or structural, aspects of the system and dynamic, or behavioral, aspects. Chapters 3 and 6 discuss the static/structural aspects of this view; Chapters 5, 7, 8, and 9 describe the dynamic/behavioral aspects.

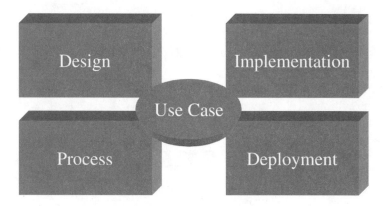

Figure 1-4: Five Views of a System

The **process view** focuses on those aspects of the system that involve timing and the flow of control. Elements of this view also address issues such as performance, scalability, and throughput. Chapters 5 and 7 contain material relevant to this view.

The **implementation view** focuses on the things that the project team assembles to form the physical system. This includes the source code, executable code, physical databases, and associated documentation, among other elements. Chapter 10 discusses these elements.

The **deployment view** focuses on the geographic distribution of the various software elements on hardware and the other physical elements that constitute the system. Chapter 10 also describes this view.

Chapter 2

The UML and Process

The UML has been designed to be independent of any particular software development process. However, its designers use three phrases that describe the key features of processes that will work best in conjunction with the UML:

- Use case driven
- Architecture-centric
- Iterative and incremental

This chapter takes a look at the basic elements of the Unified Process, which embodies these characteristics. The discussion of these elements will help you understand the UML in the larger context of the software development life cycle.

The Four Phases

The life of a software system can be represented as a series of cycles. A **cycle** ends with the release of a version of the system to customers.

Within the Unified Process, each cycle contains four phases. A **phase** is simply the span of time between two **major milestones**, points at which managers make important decisions about whether to proceed with development, and, if so, what's required concerning project scope, budget, and schedule.

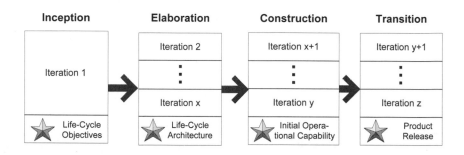

Figure 2-1: Phases and Major Milestones

Figure 2-1 shows the phases and major milestones of the Unified Process.

You can see that each phase contains one or more iterations. We'll explore the concept of iterations in the section Iterations and Increments later in this chapter.

The following subsections describe the key aspects of each of these phases.

Inception

The primary goal of the **Inception phase** is to establish the case for the viability of the proposed system.

The tasks that a project team performs during Inception include the following:

- Defining the scope of the system (that is, what's in and what's out)
- Outlining a **candidate architecture**, which is made up of initial versions of six different models
- Identifying critical risks and determining when and how the project will address them
- Starting to make the business case that the project is worth doing, based on initial estimates of cost, effort, schedule, and product quality

The candidate architecture relates to the views of a system that were described in Chapter 1 (see "Views of a System"). The six models are covered in the next major section of this chapter, "The Five Workflows."

The major milestone associated with the Inception phase is called **Life-Cycle Objectives**. The indications that the project has reached this milestone include the following:

- The major stakeholders agree on the scope of the proposed system.
- The candidate architecture clearly addresses a set of critical high-level requirements.
- The business case for the project is strong enough to justify a green light for continued development.

Chapter 4 describes how the UML addresses the task of capturing requirements.

Elaboration

The primary goal of the **Elaboration phase** is to establish the ability to build the new system given the financial constraints, schedule constraints, and other kinds of constraints that the development project faces.

The tasks that a project team performs during Elaboration include the following:

- Capturing a healthy majority of the remaining functional requirements
- Expanding the candidate architecture into a full architectural baseline, which is an internal release of the system focused on describing the architecture
- Addressing significant risks on an ongoing basis
- Finalizing the business case for the project, and preparing a project plan that contains detail sufficient to guide the next phase of the project (Construction)

The **architectural baseline** contains expanded versions of the six models initialized during the Inception phase. The UML is considered architecture-centric because of the centrality of the architectural baseline in software development efforts that use the language.

 See "Views of a System" in Chapter 1 for more about software architecture.

The major milestone associated with the Elaboration phase is called **Life-Cycle Architecture**. The indications that the project has reached this milestone include the following:

- Most of the functional requirements for the new system have been captured in the use case model.

- The architectural baseline is a small, skinny system that will serve as a solid foundation for ongoing development.

- The business case has received a green light, and the project team has an initial project plan that describes how the Construction phase will proceed.

The use case model is described in the upcoming section "The Five Workflows." Risks are discussed in the section "Iterations and Increments" later in this chapter.

Construction

The primary goal of the **Construction phase** is to build a system that is capable of operating successfully in beta customer environments.

The tasks that a project team performs during Construction involve building the system iteratively and incrementally (see Iterations and Increments later in this chapter), making sure that the viability of the system is always evident in executable form.

The major milestone associated with the Construction phase is called **Initial Operational Capability**. The project has reached this milestone if a set of beta customers has a more or less fully operational system in their hands.

Transition

The primary goal of the **Transition phase** is to roll out the fully functional system to customers.

The tasks that a project team performs during Transition focus on correcting defects and modifying the system to correct previously unidentified problems.

The major milestone associated with the Transition phase is called **Product Release**.

The Five Workflows

Within the Unified Process, five workflows cut across the set of four phases. Each **workflow** is a set of activities that various project workers perform.

The following subsections describe the key features of these workflows in terms of the kinds of UML models associated with each workflow, and also the relationship of each workflow with each of the four phases.

Requirements

The primary activities of the **Requirements workflow** are aimed at building the **use case model**, which captures the functional requirements of the system being modeled. This model allows the project stakeholders to agree on the capabilities of the system and the conditions to which it must conform.

The use case model also serves as the foundation for all other development work. Figure 2-2 shows how the use case model influences the other five UML models discussed in the subsequent subsections.

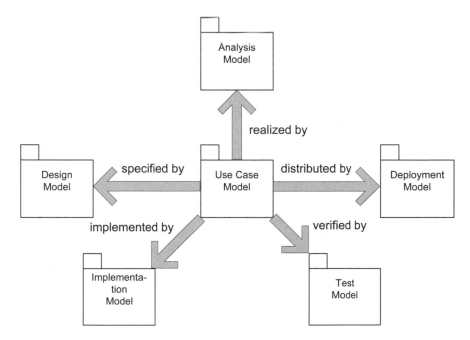

Figure 2-2: The Six Basic Unified Process Models

Chapter 4, Capturing Requirements, describes the contents of the use case model. (Chapter 3, Identifying Relevant Real-World Things, discusses how one goes about building the vocabulary that the use case model uses.) Chapters 5 through 10 explore how use cases influence the elements of the other models that get built during system development.

The use case model sits at the center of the use case view of a system's architecture.

> See "Views of a System" in Chapter 1 for more about the five views of a system's architecture defined by the UML.

Note that prototyping activities, whether they involve line drawings, full-blown working prototypes, or something in between, also are part of the Requirements workflow.

The Requirements workflow cuts across the four phases of the Unified Process roughly as follows:

- A relatively bare-bones use case model evolves during Inception, in order to capture critical high-level requirements.

- The majority (perhaps 80 percent) of the use case model gets built during Elaboration, as functional requirements are addressed on a broad basis.

- Construction generally includes building the rest of the use case model, since it's likely that some requirements weren't captured during Inception and Elaboration.

- The use case model tends to be fine-tuned during Transition.

Analysis

The primary activities of the **Analysis workflow** are aimed at building the **analysis model**, which helps the developers refine and structure the functional requirements captured within the use case model. This model contains realizations of use cases that lend themselves better than the use cases to design and implementation work.

Chapter 3, Identifying Relevant Real-World Things, discusses the beginnings of the analysis model. Chapter 5, Expressing How Things Work Together, describes how the analysis model gets fleshed out.

The analysis model participates in both the design view and the process view of the architecture.

The Analysis workflow cuts across the four phases of the Unified Process roughly as follows:

- The analysis model starts evolving during Inception, as part of the effort to represent high-level requirements.

- A large majority of the analysis model gets built during Elaboration, as functional requirements are analyzed, refined, and structured.

- Construction generally includes building the rest of the analysis model, to address unanalyzed requirements that turn up after Elaboration.

- The analysis model tends to be fine-tuned during Transition.

Design

The primary activities of the **Design workflow** are aimed at building the **design model**, which describes the physical realizations of the use cases, from the use case model, and also the contents of the analysis model. The design model serves as an abstraction of the implementation model (see the next subsection).

Chapter 5, Expressing How Things Work Together, and Chapter 6, Refining the Structure of Things, describe the key contents of the design model. (Chapters 7 through 9 describe other kinds of elements that may be part of the design model.)

The Design workflow also focuses on the **deployment model**, which defines the physical organization of the system in terms of computational nodes. Chapter 10, Describing How Things Will Be Built, addresses the deployment model.

The design model sits at the center of the design view of the architecture; it is also very relevant to the process view. Similarly, the deployment model is the heart of the deployment view.

The Design workflow cuts across the four phases of the Unified Process roughly as follows:

- The design model starts evolving during Inception, as part of the effort to realize high-level requirements. The deployment model generally consists of a few broad sketches.

- The architecturally significant use cases are addressed within the design model during Elaboration. If the system will be distributed to a significant extent, the deployment model starts taking shape here.
- Construction generally includes building the majority of the design model and the deployment model, as decisions are made about what software will live on which hardware node.
- The design model and the deployment model tend to be fine-tuned during Transition.

Implementation

The primary activities of the **Implementation workflow** are aimed at building the **implementation model**, which describes how the elements of the design model are packaged into software components, such as source code files, dynamic link libraries (DLLs), and Enterprise Java Beans (EJBs).

Chapter 10, Describing How Things Will Be Built, addresses the implementation model.

The implementation model is the key element of the implementation view of the system's architecture.

The Implementation workflow cuts across the four phases of the Unified Process roughly as follows:

- During Inception, the implementation model, if it exists, generally takes the form of an executable prototype.
- The Elaboration version of the implementation model again addresses the architecturally significant use cases.
- Construction focuses on building the large majority of the implementation model.
- The implementation model is fine-tuned during Transition.

Test

The primary activities of the **Test workflow** are aimed at building the **test model**, which describes how integration and system tests will exercise executable components from the implementation model. The test model also describes how the team will perform those tests as well as unit tests.

The test model contains test cases that are often derived directly from use cases. Testers perform black-box testing using the original use case text, and white-box testing of the realizations of those use cases, as specified within the analysis model.

Chapter 4, Capturing Requirements, discusses the test model in terms of black-box testing. Chapter 5, Expressing How Things Work Together, discusses white-box testing.

The Test workflow cuts across the four phases of the Unified Process roughly as follows:

- During Inception, the test model focuses on the executable prototype, if it exists.
- The Elaboration version of the test model again addresses the architecturally significant use cases.
- Construction focuses on building the large majority of the test model and on performing suitable unit, integration, and system testing.
- The test model is fine-tuned during Transition, as ongoing testing helps the project team uncover flaws and defects.

Iterations and Increments

As mentioned at the beginning of the chapter, each of the Unified Process's phases is divided into iterations. An **iteration** is simply a mini-project that's part of a workflow.

A typical iteration crosses all five of the workflows discussed in the previous section, to a greater or lesser extent. For instance, an iteration during the Elaboration phase might focus heavily on activities of the Requirements and Analysis workflows, whereas an iteration during Construction is more likely to involve Design, Implementation, and Test activities.

Each iteration results in an **increment**. This is a release of the system that contains added and/or improved functionality over and above the previous release.

Figure 2-3 shows the essence of the iterative and incremental approach to software development.

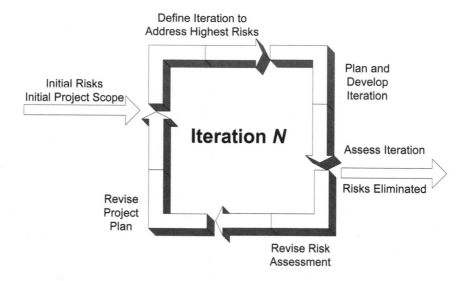

Figure 2-3: Iterative and Incremental Development

Using an iterative and incremental approach, you start the development process by evaluating your risks, including those associated with requirements,
skills, technology, and politics, and by ensuring that you define the scope of
the project to everyone's satisfaction (see "Elaboration"). Then you proceed
as follows:

1. Define the first iteration such that you address your most critical and diffi-
    cult risks. (In other words, do the hard stuff first.)

2. Map out a plan for the iteration to a suitable level of detail.

3. Perform the appropriate activities; for the Unified Process, these are
    activities associated with the Requirements, Analysis, Design, Implemen-
    tation, and Test workflows.

4. Do a postmortem on the increment that results from the iteration.

5. Discard the risks that the increment has sufficiently addressed. Then
    update your ongoing risk list.

6. Revise your overall project plan in response to the relative success or fail-
    ure of the iteration.

7. Proceed with the next iteration.

Iterations build the six models increment by increment. At the end of each iteration, the full set of models that represents the system is in a particular state; this is the architectural baseline.

 See "The Five Workflows" for information about the six Unified Process models. See "Elaboration" for more about the architectural baseline.

Chapter 3

Identifying Relevant Real-World Things

Let's begin our look at the details of the UML by exploring how we do basic modeling of things and concepts from the real world, which results in the foundation for a project glossary.

Objects

An **object** is simply a real-world thing or concept.

Suppose you're standing at an ATM getting money. The relevant objects include your ATM card, the checking account from which you're making a withdrawal, and the crisp $20 bill that you're taking from the machine. (You can think of the ATM itself as being an object as well, but an ATM is considerably more complicated than the other objects I've just identified, so I'm going to avoid discussing it.)

There are three essential aspects of objects.

- An object has *identity*. This generally takes the form of a human-readable name, but an object can also be anonymous (although in that case, it will have a name known to some computer).

- An object has *state*. This includes the names of the various properties that describe the object (its **attributes**) and also the values of those attributes at some point in time.

- An object has *behavior*. This is represented by functions, referred to as **methods**, that use or change the values of the object's attributes.

One of the fundamental principles of object orientation (OO) is that of data hiding: an object hides its data from the rest of the world and only lets outsiders manipulate that data by way of calls to the object's methods. The formal term for this is **encapsulation**.

Table 3-1 shows some attributes that are likely to belong to the objects we're discussing, and typical values for those attributes

Table 3-1: Objects, Attributes, and Values

Object	Attribute	Value
ATM Card	PIN	4321
Checking Account	ID overdraftLimit	404-2222-5582 1000
$20 Bill	serialNumber	J21097667A

Since an object can perform functions on itself, we can deduce that our ATM Card object will have a method called something like *validatePIN*, and Checking Account will have a *withdraw* method. (The $20 Bill may know how to dispense itself, but that's probably not relevant to you when you're standing at the ATM.)

It's generally accepted practice to name attributes and methods using all lowercase letters for the first word and initial caps for subsequent words. If you have an acronym (such as PIN, for personal identification number), it usually appears in all caps.

As important as objects are, though, the most important building block of any object-oriented system is the class.

Classes

A **class** is a collection of objects that have the same characteristics.

Let's compare a class with an object based on the essential aspects of an object that were defined in the previous section.

- A class has identity in the form of a human-readable name that's unique in a particular context (for instance, ATM Card or Checking Account). An object's name, if it's human readable, may include the name of the class to which the object belongs. (Object names are discussed more later in this chapter.)

- A class doesn't have state like an object does. However, a class defines attributes that belong to each object of that class.

- A class defines behavior in terms of operations, as opposed to methods. An **operation** represents a service that an object can request to affect behavior; a method is an implementation of that service. Each operation of a given class is represented by at least one method within each of the objects belonging to that class.

An object that belongs to a particular class is often referred to as an **instance** of that class. You might think of a class as being an abstraction and an object as the concrete manifestation of that abstraction.

Within the UML, the standard notation for a class is a box with three compartments, as shown in Figure 3-1.

The top compartment contains the name of the class, the middle compartment contains the attributes that belong to the class, and the bottom compartment contains the class's operations. You can, however, show a class without its attributes or its operations, or the name of the class can appear by itself (see Figure 3-2).

Figure 3-1: UML Class Notation

Figure 3-2: Alternate UML Class Notations

It's time to start talking about The Internet Bookstore. From this point forward, a healthy number of the figures in this book will refer to various aspects of models that a project team might produce in the process of building an online bookstore.

Figure 3-3 shows some of the classes associated with our bookstore.

Notice that the *title* attribute of the Book class has an associated data type (String), whereas the other three attributes in the figure don't have types. Note also that each of the three operations has a different appearance. Chapter 6 explains the various kinds of details you can attach to attributes and operations.

It's often desirable to define explicit **responsibilities** for a class. These represent the obligations that one class has with regard to other classes. Figure 3-4 shows how you can use an extra compartment within a UML class box to indicate responsibilities for one of our bookstore's classes.

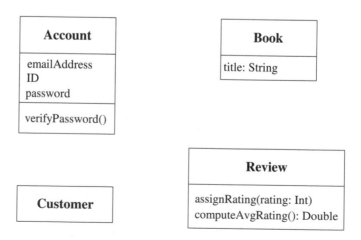

Figure 3-3: Sample Classes

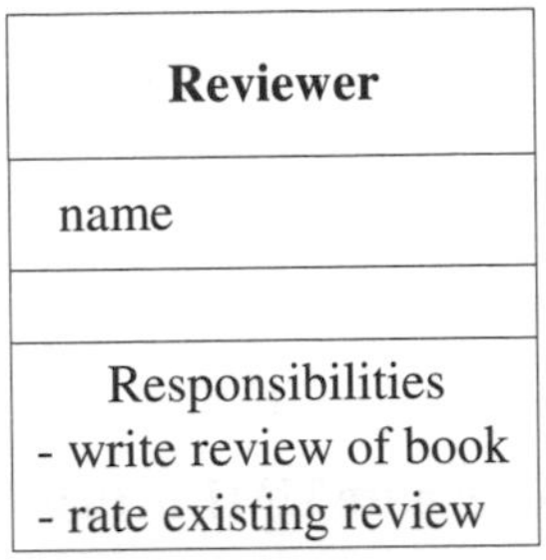

Reviewer
name
Responsibilities - write review of book - rate existing review

Figure 3-4: Class Responsibilities

As development proceeds, responsibilities tend to get explicitly addressed by operations as classes get refined. So, you shouldn't be surprised if you don't see the responsibility compartment in later versions of models that include class boxes.

Note that you can also extend a class box with other compartments that contain whatever information you want to see.

Class Relationships

Classes, by themselves, aren't particularly useful. It's the relationships among classes that provide the foundation for the structure of a new system. The following subsections explore how you use the UML to illustrate three kinds of class relationships.

Associations

An **association** is a structural connection between classes. You show an association between two classes with a straight line that connects them (see Figure 3-5).

Figure 3-6 shows some associations between classes within our current model of The Internet Bookstore.

An association is assumed to be bidirectional, which means you can navigate from either class to the other one. In other words, both classes know about each other. However, you can specify that navigation can only occur from one class to another, by using a feathered arrow, as shown in Figure 3-7.

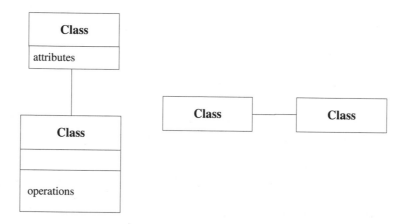

Figure 3-5: UML Association Notation

The UML also allows you to model what are called **N-ary associations**, which are relationships that involve three or more classes. This construct is most useful with regard to arenas such as data modeling, as opposed to OO modeling, so this book will not address it further.

You can add several kinds of details, or **adornments**, to an association between classes. These include the following.

• An association can have a name that indicates the nature of the relationship. If a name is present, there can also be a triangle that points in the direction in which you should read the name. See Figure 3-8.

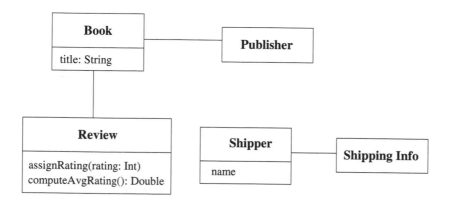

Figure 3-6: Sample Associations

Figure 3-7: One-Way Navigation between Classes

- An association can contain **roles**, which are the faces that classes present to other classes. As you can see in Figure 3-9, roles generally appear in pairs. A class can play the same role or different roles within different associations.

- An association can show **multiplicity**. This indicates how many objects associated with each class can be present within the association. The multiplicity expression can take several forms, including the following:

  – a fixed value (such as 1 or 3)

  – an asterisk (*), which means "many"

  – a range of values (for instance, 0..1 or 3..*)

  – a set of values (for example, 1, 3, 5, 7)

  Figure 3-10 shows two examples of association multiplicity. When an association has multiplicities attached to it, you read from a class to the value next to the other class across the association. So, in the figure, one Account can be connected with many Billing Info objects, but each Billing Info object is connected with only one Account.

Aggregation

An **aggregation** is a special kind of association—a "whole/part" relationship within which one or more smaller classes are "parts" of a larger "whole."

Using the UML, you show an aggregation by using a line with an open diamond at one end. The class next to the diamond is the "whole" class; the class at the other end of the line is the "part" class. See Figure 3-11.

Figure 3-8: Named Association

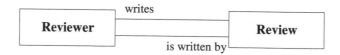

Figure 3-9: Association Roles

If a given class aggregates more than one class, you can show each aggregation using a separate line, or you can consolidate the lines. Figure 3-12 shows both variations. A class can also aggregate itself, as shown in Figure 3-13.

The self-aggregation construct is useful in situations such as those that involve "rollups" for reporting purposes.

Figure 3-14 shows aggregations that exist for our online bookstore, with the diamonds pointing to the "whole" Order.

Note that multiplicities now appear on each aggregation relationship. If an aggregation doesn't show multiplicity values, the default is many (*) "parts" and one "whole."

Generalization

Generalization refers to a relationship between a general class (the **superclass** or **parent**) and a more specific version of that class (the **subclass** or **child**). You can think of the subclass as being a kind of the superclass.

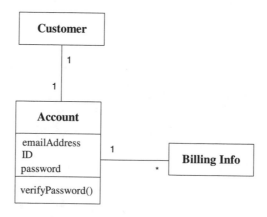

Figure 3-10: Association Multiplicity

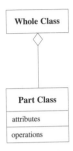

Figure 3-11: UML Aggregation Notation

A subclass **inherits** the attributes and operations from one superclass (this is called **single inheritance**) or from more than one superclass (**multiple inheritance**).

Inheritance is one of the key features of OO. Two more important principles associated with generalization are as follows:

- The principle of **substitutability** states that an object of a subclass may be substituted anywhere an object of an associated superclass is used.

- The principle of **polymorphism** states that an object of a subclass can redefine any of the operations it inherits from its superclass(es).

An object belonging to a subclass can also add attributes or operations or both to the ones it inherits.

The UML notation for a generalization is a line with an open triangle at one end. The class next to the diamond is the parent/superclass; the class at the other end of the line is the child/subclass. See Figure 3-15.

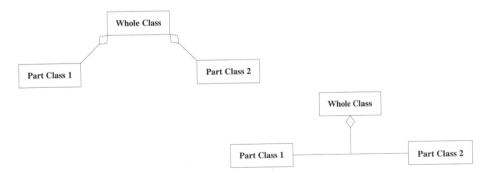

Figure 3-12: Aggregating Multiple Classes

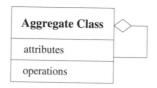

Figure 3-13: Self-Aggregation

If a given class has more than one child/subclass, you can show each generalization using a separate line, or you can consolidate the lines, as with aggregation. Figure 3-16 shows both variations.

Figure 3-17 shows a generalization that exists for The Internet Bookstore. Notice the change from Figure 3-6: the operations that used to belong to the Review class have been pushed down into Customer Review. This is because these methods don't apply to the new Editorial Review class. This is a good example of how the subclass, Customer Review, specializes the more general superclass, Review.

Association Classes

An **association class** is a cross between an association and a class. You use it to model an association that has interesting characteristics of its own outside the classes it connects.

This construct also comes in handy when you have a many-to-many relationship that you'd like to break into a set of one-to-many relationships.

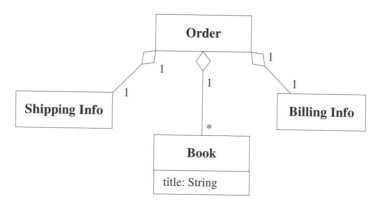

Figure 3-14: Sample Aggregations

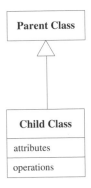

Figure 3-15: UML Generalization Notation

You represent an association class itself with a regular class box; you indicate that it's an association class by connecting it to the association between the other two classes using a dashed line. See Figure 3-18.

Figure 3-19 shows an association class present within the model for our online bookstore. In this case, there would normally be a many-to-many relationship between Author and Book, because an Author may have written more than one Book, and a Book may have more than one Author. The presence of the BookAndAuthor association class allows us to pair one Author with one Book; the *role* attribute gives us the option of stating whether the Author was the primary author, supporting author, editor, or whatever.

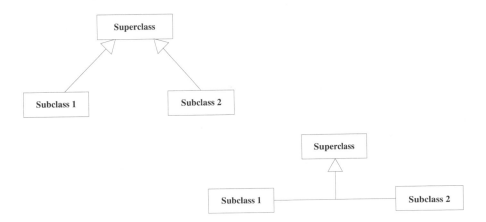

Figure 3-16: Generalizing Multiple Classes

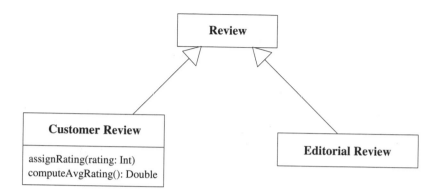

Figure 3-17: Sample Generalization

Class Diagrams

A **class diagram** shows classes and the various relationships in which they are involved. Class diagrams are the primary means by which you show the structure of a system being developed.

Figure 3-20 shows a class diagram that includes most of the classes and relationships we've looked at so far for our online bookstore. Note that this diagram doesn't show all of the logical associations that would be present in the model at this stage. For instance, Customer and Order should certainly be connected, since only a Customer can place an Order. You would also expect to see an association between Customer and Reviewer, since a Customer can also be a Reviewer.

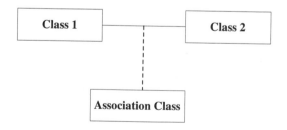

Figure 3-18: UML Association Class Notation

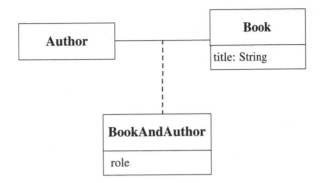

Figure 3-19: Sample Association Class

These associations are absent from the diagram intentionally, both because the diagram is fairly rich already and because a class diagram doesn't have to explicitly show every possible connection between classes. In this case, you can see that Customer has relationships with both Reviewer and Order by way of other classes, which is sufficient for our purposes. In Chapter 6, we'll look at a class diagram that offers more details.

Object Diagrams

The UML notation for an object takes the same basic form as that for a class. There are three differences:

- Within the top compartment of the class box, the name of the class to which the object belongs appears after a colon. The object may have a name, which appears before the colon, or it may be anonymous, in which case nothing appears before the colon.

- The contents of the top compartment are underlined for an object.

- Each attribute defined for the given class has a specific value for each object that belongs to that class.

Figure 3-21 shows the UML notation for both a named object and an anonymous object.

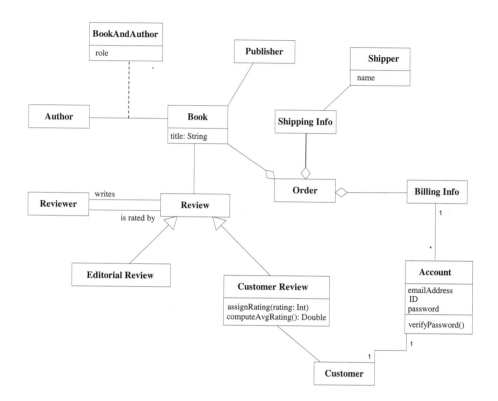

Figure 3-20: Class Diagram

An **object diagram** is basically a snapshot of part of the structure of the system being modeled. It has the same basic appearance as a class diagram, except that it shows objects, and actual values for attributes, instead of classes.

Figure 3-22 shows an object diagram for The Internet Bookstore.

Figure 3-21: UML Object Notation

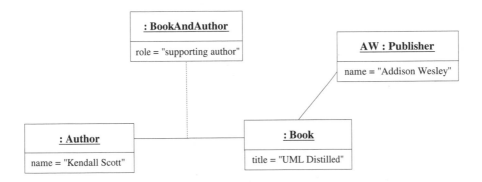

Figure 3-22: Sample Object Diagram

As you can see, only one of the four objects has a name. It's fairly common for many objects in a system to remain anonymous.

Notes

You can use **notes** as adornments on class diagrams and object diagrams to record a comment for a specific class or object, a set of classes or objects, or a diagram as a whole.

Notes do not have any impact on the model you're building. They're simply there to facilitate communication. For instance, someone might attach a note to a class posting a question to a reviewer, while another note might indicate that the set of classes shown on a particular class diagram is likely to be part of some future release of the system.

Although a note generally has text, you might also see a note with something like a small graphic or a hyperlink to another document.

A note, which the UML represents as a rectangle with the upper right-hand corner folded down, can appear anywhere on any kind of UML diagram. Alternatively, you might see a note attached to a particular element of a diagram, such as a class on a class diagram. Figure 3-23 shows the formats of both types of notes.

Figure 3-24 shows some notes for our online bookstore.

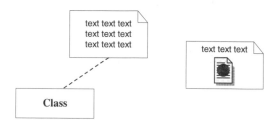

Figure 3-23: UML Notes

It's common practice to simply remove a note from a diagram when the question it poses, or the issue it raises, has been addressed. In the case of our sample notes, once the project team has decided whether to specialize the Reviewer class and change the multiplicity on the association between Customer and Account, the notes will disappear.

Packages

A **package** is a grouping of pieces of a model. Packages are very useful in managing models. They're also quite helpful in grouping related items in order to make it easier to break work up among subteams.

A package can contain one or more kinds of model elements. You can have just classes in a package, for instance, or classes and class diagrams, or a number of different kinds of constructs and diagrams. The only rule is that each element of a model can belong to only one package. Note, though, that a package is a *conceptual* grouping; the system will not be built along package boundaries.

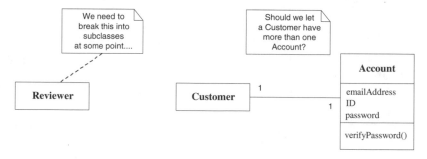

Figure 3-24: Sample Notes

Figure 3-25: UML Packages

In UML terms, a model is basically a package that contains other packages. An analysis model, for instance (see Analysis in Chapter 1), is likely to contain a number of packages of classes. Many of the classes represented within the analysis model will be connected with the classes that a development team "discovers" during the early stages of a project, as Chapter 5 will explore.

You show a UML package as a tabbed folder. There are two variations:

- The name of the package appears within the tab, and the contents of the package are listed in the body of the folder.
- The package name appears in the body of the folder, and the contents are hidden from view.

Figure 3-25 shows both kinds of package notation. If this notation looks familiar, it's because it appeared in Figure 2-2, which showed the six basic Unified Process models.

Figure 3-26 shows some packages of classes for our bookstore.

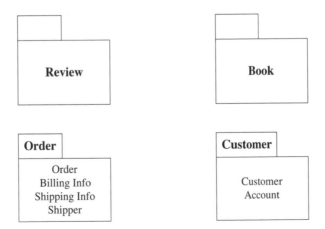

Figure 3-26: Sample Packages

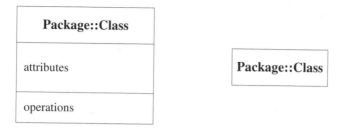

Figure 3-27: Class Path Name Notation

The name of a class can include the package to which it belongs, as shown in Figure 3-27. This extended form of the name of a class is called the **path name** of the class. A path name can also include the package(s) that enclose the package to which the given class directly belongs, with the "outermost" package appearing first in the name. Figure 3-28 shows path names for two of our sample classes.

We'll be looking at packages associated with The Internet Bookstore throughout the rest of the book. Some of these packages will contain only one kind of model element, whereas others will contain a mixture of elements.

The term **domain model** is often used to describe the set of classes that come out of the early stages of a development project. In the next chapter, we'll see how to use the classes contained within the domain model in the context of functional requirements.

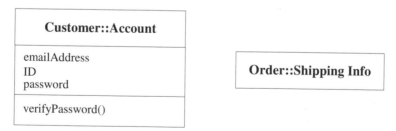

Figure 3-28: Sample Classes with Path Names

Chapter 4

Capturing Requirements

The task of capturing the requirements associated with a new system is a complicated one, and one that never seems to stop. In this chapter, we'll look at how we can use the UML to make the job easier. The chapter also explains how we can use the project "glossary" discussed in the previous chapter to advantage in the context of this effort.

Chapter 2 stated that one of the key tenets of the UML is its use-case-driven nature. It also mentioned that the use case model, which allows the project stakeholders to agree on what the system should do, serves as the foundation for all other development work. Let's explore the elements of this model.

Actors and Use Cases

An **actor** represents one of two things:

- A role that a user can play with regard to a system
- An entity, such as another system or a database, that resides outside the system

You show an actor as a stick figure with a short descriptive name, as illustrated in Figure 4-1.

Actor

Figure 4-1: UML Actor Notation

Note that the name of an actor should *not* be that of a particular person; instead, it should identify a role or set of roles that a human being, an external system, or a part of the system being built will play relative to one or more use cases.

Figure 4-2 shows some of the human and nonhuman actors that interact with The Internet Bookstore.

A user can serve as more than one type of actor. For example, in our bookstore, a Customer can buy books, or he or she can write Customer Reviews (see Figure 3-17).

A **use case** is a sequence of actions that an actor performs within a system to achieve a particular goal.

A good use case is expressed from the viewpoint of the actor, in present tense and active voice. We'll explore this further in the next section. A use case should describe one aspect of usage of the system without presuming any specific design or implementation. In other words, a use case describes *what* the system needs to do without specifying *how* the system will perform.

You show a use case as an ellipse with a short name that contains an active verb and (usually) a noun phrase. As you can see in Figure 4-3, the name of a use case can appear either within the ellipse or below it.

Customer   Shipping System   Accountant

Figure 4-2: Sample Actors

Figure 4-3: Use Case Notation

The total set of actors within a use case model (see Requirements in Chapter 2) should reflect everything that needs to exchange information with the system being modeled. The total set of use cases within that model should capture all of the functional requirements that the system's stakeholders have put forth.

Figure 4-4 shows some of the use cases for our bookstore.

Use Case Diagrams

You show actors and use cases on **use case diagrams**.

- The actor that executes a given use case usually appears on the left-hand side of the diagram.
- The use cases appear in the center.
- Any other actors that are involved in the given use cases tend to appear on the right-hand side.
- Arrows show which actors are involved in which use cases.

Figure 4-5 shows how actors and use cases appear on a UML use case diagram.

Within the diagram, Actor 1 is involved in the execution of all three use cases, and Actor 3 is also actively involved in Use Case 3, but Actor 2 is merely the recipient of something associated with Use Case 2.

Figure 4-4: Sample Use Cases

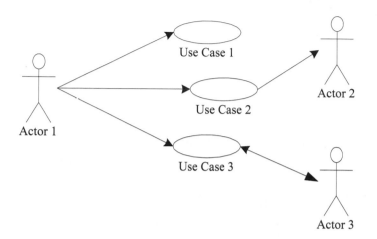

Figure 4-5: Use Case Diagram

Figure 4-6 shows a use case diagram for The Internet Bookstore. This diagram shows only relationships between the actor and the use cases; we'll look at relationships that can exist between use cases later in this chapter.

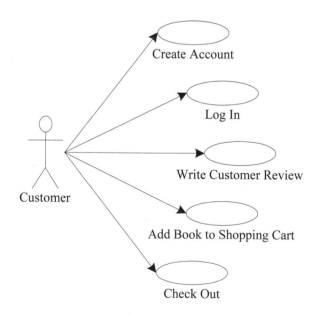

Figure 4-6: Sample Use Case Diagram

Flows of Events

The text of a use case describes possible paths through the use case. This text includes the actions that the actor performs and the system's responses to those actions. (I like to describe this in terms of "call and response.") You capture these paths as flows of events.

Two kinds of flows of events are associated with use cases.

- The **main flow of events** (sometimes referred to as the **basic course of action**) is the sunny-day scenario, the main start-to-finish path that the actor and the system will follow under normal circumstances. The assumption is that the primary actor doesn't make any mistakes, and the system generates no errors. A use case always has a main flow of events.

- An **exceptional flow of events** (or **alternate course of action**) is a path through a use case that represents an error condition or a path that the actor and the system take less frequently. A use case often has at least one exceptional flow of events; in fact, the more interesting behavior described by use cases is often found in the alternate courses.

The text for the basic course of action for a use case is typically between one and three paragraphs long; text for alternate courses tends to be a sentence or two for each course. The idea is for each use case to address one or more requirements in text that's easy to understand quickly for everyone involved in the project, whether technically savvy or not. (Note that it may be the case that more than one use case is necessary to capture a requirement.)

Let's look at a couple of use cases for The Internet Bookstore. We'll start by walking through how a use case named Log In might have come into existence.

The first step is to establish where the actor is, and what he or she does to initiate the use case:

> The Customer clicks the Login button on the Home Page.

The use case then describes the system's response:

> The system displays the Login Page.

The rest of the basic course of action for this use case describes the actions that the actor performs in order to log in to the bookstore, and the actions that the system performs along the way as well:

> The Customer enters his or her user ID and password, and then clicks the OK button. The system validates the login information against the persistent Account data, and then returns the Customer to the Home Page.

Remember that the Account class we defined in Chapter 3 (see Figure 3-3) contains three attributes, two of which are *ID* and *password*. It's good practice to make explicit connections to domain model classes within use case text.

As you can see, the basic course addresses the mainstream path, and it also assumes that nothing will go wrong. However, a good use case accounts for as many alternate paths and error conditions as possible. In this case, there are two kinds of alternate courses that we need to address.

- The Customer can perform some other action before logging in. This leads to these alternate courses:

> If the Customer clicks the New Account button, the system displays the Create New Account page.

> If the Customer clicks the Reminder Word button, the system displays a dialog box containing the reminder word stored for that Customer. When the Customer clicks the OK button, the system returns the Customer to the Home Page.

- The system is unable to validate a value that the Customer provided, and thus is unable to complete the login process. The following courses of action are possible:

> If the Customer enters a user ID that the system does not recognize, the system displays the Create New Account page.

> If the Customer enters an incorrect password, the system prompts the Customer to reenter his or her password.

> If the Customer enters an incorrect password three times, the system displays a page telling the Customer that he or she should contact customer service.

The reader of a use case should be able to see where each alternate course branches out from the basic course. Log In is short enough that this isn't an issue, but longer or more complicated use cases may pose problems in this area. Some people like to number the steps of the basic course and then use the appropriate numbers as references within the alternate courses.

One of the key principles of a use case is that it has to end with the system providing some result of value to an actor. The basic course of Log In reflects that the Customer is logged in to the system at the end. The alternate courses also reflect that result, albeit in somewhat different ways. In two cases, the Customer ends up back at the Home Page, and the assumption is that he or she will proceed with the basic course of action. In another case, the system takes the Customer to a different page; this may not be a desirable option from his or her standpoint, but it's still a result of value. And in two cases, the system displays a new page that the Customer can use to create a new account. (Let's assume that some use case diagram for The Internet Bookstore will show that Log In has a connection with a Create New Account use case.)

Our second, more complicated, use case is called Write Customer Review. It illustrates the basic principles this chapter has presented: active voice from the actor's perspective, present tense, a result of value, and alternate courses of action that reflect different paths.

Basic Course

> The Customer presses the Review This Book button on the Book Page. The system displays a page entitled Write a Review.

> The Customer selects a rating for the given Book, types a title for his or her review, and then types the review itself. Then the Customer indicates whether the system should display his or her name or E-mail address, or both, in connection with the review.

> When the Customer has finished selecting and entering information, he or she presses the Preview My Review button. The system displays a Look Over Your Review page that contains the information that the Customer provided. The Customer presses the Save button. The system stores the information associated with the Review and returns the Customer to the Book Page.

Alternate Courses

> If the Customer presses the Review Guidelines button on the Book Page, the system displays the Customer Review Guidelines page. When the Customer presses the OK button on that page, the system returns the Customer to the Book Page.

> If the Customer presses the Edit button on the Look Over My Review page, the system allows the Customer to make changes to any of the information that he or she provided on the Write a Review page. When the Customer presses the Save button, the system stores the review information and returns the Customer to the Book Page.

This chapter has spent so much time on use cases because they represent the fundamental negotiating tool available to the participants in a software development project. The net result of a robust set of use cases (in other words, the full use case model) is something of a contractual agreement between the developers and the other stakeholders—and when it comes to requirements, we all know just how much negotiating needs to take place for a typical project.

Organizing Use Cases

It's likely that a significant part of the effort to build a use case model will involve breaking up use cases in search of simpler ones. The UML offers three constructs for factoring out common behavior and variant paths. The following subsections describe these constructs.

Include

Within an **include** relationship, one use case *explicitly* includes the behavior of another use case at a specified point within a course of action.

The included use case doesn't stand alone; it has to be connected with one or more base use cases. The include mechanism is very useful for factoring out behavior that would otherwise appear within multiple use cases.

Figure 4-7 shows how the UML represents an include relationship.

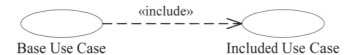

Figure 4-7: Include Notation

The symbols around the word "include" are called "guillemets." An explanation of their special meaning within the UML appears in Chapter 6. That chapter also discusses the dashed arrow introduced in Figure 4-7.

Within Figure 4-8, the Add to Wish List and Check Out use cases include the behavior captured within the Log In use case because a Customer of The Internet Bookstore must be logged in before he or she can add a book to a wish list or make a purchase.

Extend

Within an **extend** relationship, a base use case *implicitly* includes the behavior of another use case at one or more specified points. These points are called **extension points**.

You generally use this construct to factor out behavior that's optional or that occurs only under certain conditions. One way to use "extends" is in creating a new use case in response to an alternate course of action having several steps associated with it.

Figure 4-9 shows the UML notation for the extend relationship.

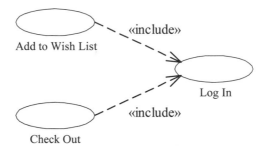

Figure 4-8: Sample Include Relationships

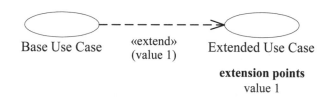

Figure 4-9: Extend Notation

Figure 4-10 shows that a Customer of our bookstore has the option of canceling an Order in conjunction with checking the status of that Order.

Use Case Generalization

Generalization works the same way for use cases as it does for classes (see Generalization in Chapter 3): a parent use case defines behavior that its children can inherit, and the children can add to or override that behavior. As you can see from Figure 4-11, the UML shows use case generalization using the same open triangle as for class generalization.

As with classes, if a given use case has more than one child, you can show each generalization with a separate line, or you can consolidate the lines. Figure 4-12 shows both variations.

Figure 4-13 shows use cases that describe three different searches that a bookstore Customer can perform, all of which use the basic search technique defined by the Perform Search use case.

Packages and Use Cases

Chapter 3 introduced the concept of the package and provided examples of packages that held only classes. Packages of related use cases (see Figure 4-14) are often very helpful in dividing work among subteams.

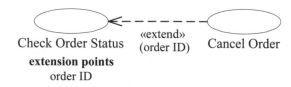

Figure 4-10: Sample Extend Relationship

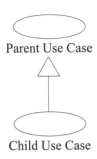

Figure 4-11: Use Case Generalization Notation

The use case model is basically a package of use case packages. As discussed in Chapter 2, the use case model influences all of the other core models identified by the Unified Process. Here's what we'll see in subsequent chapters about the nature of this influence:

- Chapter 5, Expressing How Things Work Together, describes how the analysis model contains realizations of use cases. These realizations express use cases in more detail, using the language of developers rather than the more generic language of the use cases. The realizations also represent the initial allocation of the behavior specified by the use cases to specific objects.

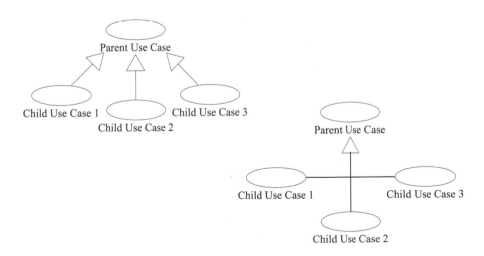

Figure 4-12: Generalizing Multiple Use Cases

Figure 4-13: Sample Use Case Generalization

- Chapter 5 also describes elements of the design model, as does Chapter 6, Refining the Structure of Things, which talks about design-level classes. Chapters 7 through 9 also discuss elements that may be part of the design model. The use case model and the analysis model together provide the foundation for the design model.

- Chapter 10, Describing How Things Will Be Built, describes key aspects of the implementation model and the deployment model. Within a well-executed project, these aspects will have fairly obvious connections to use cases.

Figure 4-15 shows the contents of a use case package for our online bookstore.

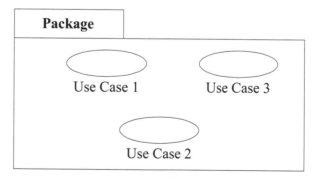

Figure 4-14: Use Case Package Notation

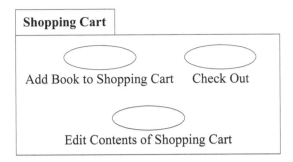

Figure 4-15: Sample Package of Use Cases

As you can see, the use cases in the Shopping Cart package are closely related to each other. Other use case packages of interest for our bookstore include Reviews, which contains the Write Customer Review use case and use cases involving Customers rating Customer Reviews and bookstore personnel writing Editorial Reviews; and Account Maintenance, which contains use cases that involve a Customer's account as well as containing the Log In use case. We'll revisit the Log In use case in the next chapter.

More about Use Cases

The following points should reinforce the importance of use cases in any modeling effort that involves the UML.

- Rapid prototyping is now well established as a technique for developers and customers to use in sitting down together and building something that will demonstrate "proof of concept." Use cases—the basic courses of action, at least—are fairly easy to build and refine as prototypes evolve.

- If you're reverse engineering an existing system, it's often useful to derive use cases from whatever user documentation is available. In fact, the organization of a user manual lends itself nicely to the design of use case packages: each chapter of the manual might correspond with a package. The procedural nature of a user guide has a direct correlation with how use cases should read.

- Use cases are also very handy with regard to testing. A quality assurance (QA) person can often pick up a package of use cases and use the basic and alternate course text more or less directly in performing black-box testing. Think of a tester as putting himself or herself in the user's shoes: the tester doesn't care how the system works, only about the results. This is how the connection between the use case model and the test model is formed.

In the next chapter, we'll start seeing the details of how use cases fuel design efforts that use the UML.

Chapter 5

Expressing How Things Work Together

We started looking at the static aspects of UML models in Chapter 3. In Chapter 4, we began to explore the dynamic aspects. In this chapter, we're going to see how modelers start looking at the static and dynamic aspects of a system in parallel, as the focus of the development effort moves to preliminary design and then detailed design.

Robustness Analysis

Robustness analysis involves analyzing the text of a use case and identifying a first-guess set of objects that will participate in the use case, and then classifying these objects based on their characteristics.

This activity is associated with the Analysis workflow within the Unified Process (see Chapter 2). You can also think of robustness analysis in terms of preliminary design. The development team starts defining what that process refers to as **analysis classes**, which are at the heart of the analysis model.

There are three types of analysis classes: **boundary classes**, **entity classes**, and **control classes**. The following subsections describe these classes in terms of the objects that serve as instances of the classes.

Figure 5-1: Boundary Object

Boundary Objects

A **boundary object** is an object with which an actor associated with a use case interacts. If the actor is human, the boundary object is likely to be a window, screen, dialog box, or menu. A nonhuman actor interacts with boundary objects such as application program interfaces (APIs). Boundary objects correspond with nouns in use case text.

Figure 5-1 shows the symbol for a boundary object.

Entity Objects

An **entity object** is generally an object that contains long-lived information, such as that associated with databases. An entity object can also contain transient data, such as the contents of lists in windows, or search results. Entity objects also correspond with nouns in use case text.

Figure 5-2 shows the symbol for an entity object.

Control Objects

A **control object** is an object that embodies application logic. Control objects are often used to handle things such as coordination and sequencing. They are also useful for calculations involving multiple entity objects.

Control objects serve as the connecting tissue between boundary objects and entity objects. They correspond with verbs in use case text.

Figure 5-3 shows the symbol for a control object.

Figure 5-2: Entity Object

Figure 5-3: Control Object

Putting Analysis Objects Together

Let's bring back our Log In use case from Chapter 4 (see the section Flows of Events). Here's the text for the basic course of action:

> The Customer clicks the Login button on the Home Page.
> The system displays the Login Page. The Customer enters his
> or her user ID and password, and then clicks the OK button.
> The system validates the login information against the persis-
> tent Account data, and then returns the Customer to the Home
> Page.

Let's walk through the creation of a **robustness diagram** for this basic course. This involves taking each sentence of the use case, determining the boundary, entity, and control objects that we'll need in order to address the behavior it specifies, and drawing those objects and their relationships. The Customer actor will appear as appropriate.

The first sentence is *The Customer clicks the Login button on the Home Page.* In addition to Customer, we need two boundary objects. Because the Login button is part of the Home Page, we can model this as an aggregation relationship (see Class Relationships in Chapter 3). Figure 5-4 shows the beginning of our robustness diagram.

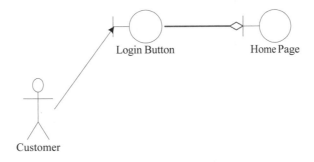

Figure 5-4: Log In Robustness Diagram, Part 1

A different modeler might choose to leave the Login button off the diagram, and instead show an arrow between the Customer and the Home Page. It's likely, in that case, that the arrow would have a label such as "clickOK" to indicate the nature of the connection.

You may be wondering why the diagram doesn't show a control object for the word "click." It's because the "click" is implicit in the connection between the Customer and the Login button, and also because, generally speaking, control objects correspond with system actions, as opposed to actions that an actor performs.

The second sentence of our basic course is *The system displays the Login Page.* We need to introduce our first control object, to represent "displays," and we have a new boundary object. Since we left off at the Home Page, let's go ahead and include that in our next chunk of the robustness diagram, captured in Figure 5-5.

By the way, it's fairly common practice to say "the system" rather than something more specific. When a team is drawing robustness diagrams, it's too early in the project to make decisions about who's doing what. As we'll see later in the chapter, that's what detailed design is for.

Robustness analysis has a set of rules about which kinds of analysis objects can talk to each other. One of these rules is that a boundary object can't talk to another boundary object, which is why the Display control object was introduced. Later in the chapter, we'll see examples of how control objects get converted to methods on other objects as design proceeds.

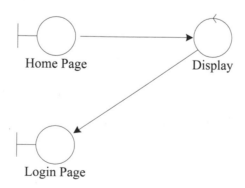

Home Page   Display

Login Page

Figure 5-5: Log In Robustness Diagram, Part 2

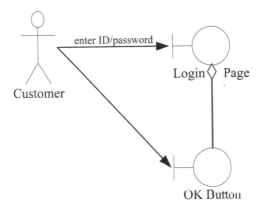

Figure 5-6: Log In Robustness Diagram, Part 3

Our third sentence for Log In is *The Customer enters his or her user ID and password, and then clicks the OK button.* So, we now have a fourth boundary object, which is part of the Login Page. Figure 5-6 shows this addition to our diagram.

The text on the arrow between Customer and Login Page is optional; it simply reinforces what appears in the text of the use case.

An interesting thing about a robustness diagram is that it's often hard to see the flow of control just by looking at the diagram, but it's easy, on a good robustness diagram, to trace the flow of the associated use case. In fact, tracing your finger through the diagram while you read the text of the use case is an excellent way to check the quality of the diagram *and* of the use case.

The fourth and last sentence of the basic course for the Log In use case is *The system validates the login information against the persistent Account data, and then returns the Customer to the Home Page.* This calls for two more objects: a control object for "validates," and our first entity object, for Account. As you may have guessed, another one of the rules of robustness analysis is that boundary objects can't talk to entity objects, so our new control object will sit between the OK button and the Account. Note also that we can "reuse" the Display control object that appears in Figure 5-5.

Figure 5-7 shows these new objects, and some objects we've already defined, as part of the final piece of the robustness diagram for Log In's basic course.

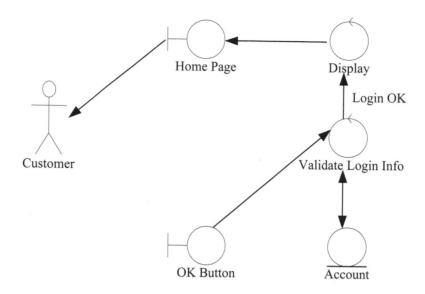

Figure 5-7: Log In Robustness Diagram, Part 4

The double-headed arrow between Validate Login Info and Account indicates that the control object expects a response from the entity object. You might see this kind of thing shown as a single-headed arrow; as long as the intent is clear, the nature of the arrow isn't important.

The label on the arrow between Validate Login Info and Display is important, though: if alternate courses appear on a robustness diagram, it's useful to label the various paths that correspond with the basic course and each of the alternate courses. In this case, the presence of "Login OK" indicates that some kind of "login failed" label will appear on an alternate path out of Validate Login Info. (The results of performing robustness analysis on Log In's alternate courses of action don't appear here for reasons of space, but you should expect to see alternate courses represented on robustness diagrams.)

Note that by showing control returning to the Customer, we've made a round trip, which confirms that the Log In use case produces a result of value to its actor.

Figure 5-8 shows the complete robustness diagram for the basic course of the Log In use case.

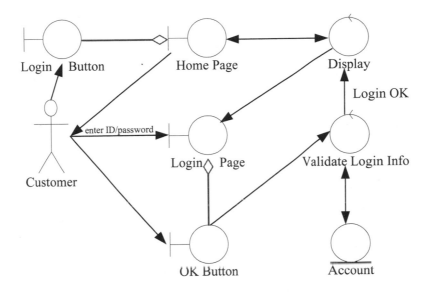

Figure 5-8: Final Log In Robustness Diagram

Later in the chapter, we'll see how a UML diagram used in detailed design evolves from this diagram. If you peek ahead, please note that the Login and OK buttons that appear here on the robustness diagram don't appear on that interaction diagram.

Note that robustness diagrams can also serve as guides for white-box testing.

Messages and Actions

The next step in modeling the dynamic behavior of a system involves modeling the interactions among objects. These interactions take the form of sets of messages.

A **message** is a communication between two objects, or within an object, that is designed to result in some activity. Generally, this activity involves one or more **actions**, which are executable statements that result in changes in the values of one or more attributes of an object or the return of some value(s) to the object that sent the message, or both.

The following subsections describe the five kinds of actions that the UML explicitly supports.

Call and Return

A **call action** is an invocation of a method on an object. A call action is synchronous, which means that the sender assumes that the receiver is ready to accept the message, and the sender waits for a response from the receiver before proceeding with the rest of its activities.

An object can perform a call action on another object, or an object can perform a call action on itself.

The UML represents a call action as an arrow from the calling object to the receiving object. Figure 5-9 shows the notation for a call action that involves two objects and a call action from an object to itself.

The dashed line that appears beneath each object in the diagram is called a **lifeline**. The explanation for this term appears in the section Sequence Diagram Notation which appears later in the chapter.

A **return action** is the return of a value in response to a call action. You show a return action as a dashed arrow from the object returning the value to the object receiving the value (in other words, from the original receiver to the original caller). See Figure 5-10.

Figure 5-11 shows two call actions and a return action relevant to The Internet Bookstore.

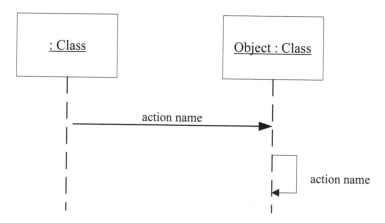

Figure 5-9: Call Action Notation

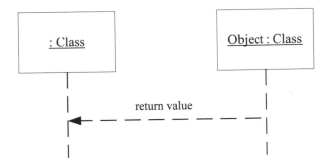

Figure 5-10: Return Action Notation

Note that you might not see a return action in connection with a send action if the return value is obvious from the context.

Create and Destroy

A **create action** creates an object. (Technically, it tells a class to create an instance of itself.) Figure 5-12 shows the UML notation for a create action.

You might also see a created object appear at the other end of the "create" arrow with a lifeline that begins after the create action occurs, as shown in Figure 5-13.

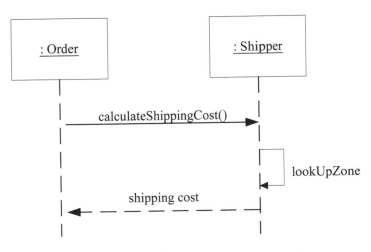

Figure 5-11: Sample Call and Return Actions

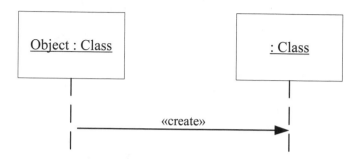

Figure 5-12: Create Action Notation

The guillemets around "create" and "destroy" indicate that these words fall into the same basic category of UML keywords as "include" and "extend" did in Chapter 4 (see Organizing Use Cases). This category is discussed in the next chapter.

A **destroy action** destroys an object. (To be precise, it tells an object to destroy itself.) An object can perform a destroy action on another object, or an object can perform a destroy action on itself. See Figure 5-14. Note that the large X at the end of the arrow results in the termination of the Account object's lifeline.

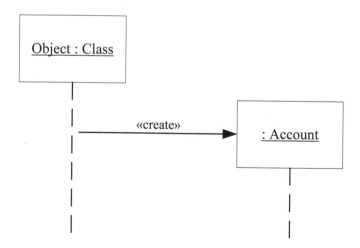

Figure 5-13: Alternate Create Action Notation

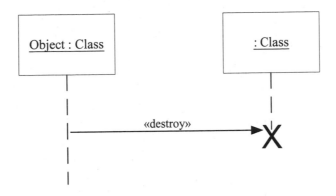

Figure 5-14: Destroy Action Notation

Send

A **send action** sends a signal to an object. A **signal** is an asynchronous communication between objects: one object "throws" a signal to another object that "catches" the signal, but the sender of the signal doesn't expect a response from the receiver, unlike the sender of a call action.

Exceptions are the most common types of signals.

Figure 5-15 shows the UML notation for a send action: an arrow with a half arrowhead at the lifeline of the receiving object.

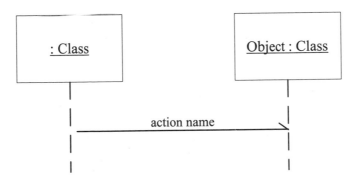

Figure 5-15: Send Action Notation

Figure 5-16 shows a send action of interest to our online bookstore.

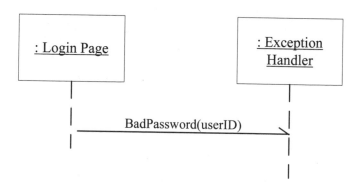

Figure 5-16: Sample Send Action

In this case, the Login Page object might have performed a destroy action on itself, since it goes away once it throws the exception.

Figure 5-17 shows how you represent a signal, and the signals that objects belonging to a given class can respond to, using UML notation.

The attributes of a signal, as defined in the attribute compartment of the class box, serve as the signal's parameters when an object sends the signal to another object. The extra compartment in a class box contains the names of signals to which objects of the given class can respond.

Figure 5-18 shows the signal that appeared in the form of a send action in Figure 5-16.

Sequence Diagrams

The UML **sequence diagram** is a diagram that focuses on the time ordering of the messages that go back and forth between objects.

Figure 5-17: Signals

Figure 5-18: Sample Signal

Sequence diagrams are also associated with the Design workflow within the Unified Process (see Chapter 2). The development team uses sequence diagrams in deciding where to assign operations on classes, based on the methods that they assign to objects on the diagram.

Sequence Diagram Notation

A sequence diagram has four key elements.

- Objects appear along the top margin. These can appear in the form described in Chapter 3 (see Object Diagrams), or they can appear as icons, as they do on robustness diagrams (see Figure 5-8).

- As mentioned earlier, each object has a **lifeline**, a dashed line that represents the life, and perhaps the death, of that object. (If there isn't a "destroy" X on the lifeline, you can assume the object is persistent.)

- A **focus of control** is a tall, thin rectangle that sits on top of an object's lifeline. The rectangle shows the period of time during which the given object is in control of the flow—for instance, when the object is executing a method or creating another object. (Note that it's optional to show focus-of-control rectangles on a sequence diagram.)

- Messages show the actions that objects perform on each other and on themselves.

Building a Sequence Diagram

Let's walk through the creation of a sequence diagram for the basic course of action of the Log In use case, using the robustness diagram for that course (see Figure 5-8) as a starting point. Actually, we'll walk through each of the pieces of that diagram (Figures 5-4 through 5-7), just like we walked through each sentence of the basic course of Log In while examining how robustness analysis is done. This process mirrors what happens in the Unified Process when the team uses the analysis model, whose primary contents are robustness diagrams, as a foundation for the design model.

 See "Analysis" in Chapter 2 for more about the analysis model. See "Design," also in Chapter 2, for more about the design model.

The first piece of the robustness diagram (Figure 5-4) contains the Customer, the Login button, and the Home Page. As mentioned previously, the buttons that appear on the robustness diagram will not appear on the sequence diagram for Log In. This is because it's easier to fold the buttons into their "aggregating" pages, which makes the sequence diagram easier to read. So, we only need to show Customer and Home Page on our new diagram.

Of course, we also need to show that the Customer clicks the Login button, which we'll express as a message from Customer to Home Page. Figure 5-19 shows the two objects and the message.

As you can see, the focus of control for Home Page starts where the focus of control for Customer ends. This is an explicit representation of how control passes from one object to another. The diagram also shows the accompanying sentence of the use case, directly across from the message. This is a good practice because it reinforces the fact that the use cases are driving the development of the system.

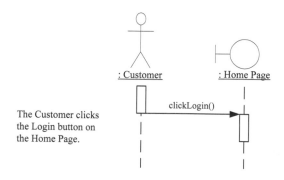

Figure 5-19: Log In Sequence Diagram, Part 1

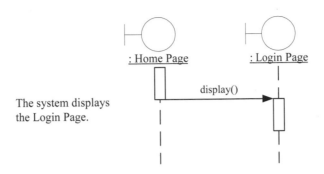

Figure 5-20: Log In Sequence Diagram, Part 2

The second piece of the robustness diagram (Figure 5-5) contains the Home Page and the Login Page, and also the Display control object. As mentioned previously, control objects often end up becoming methods on other objects; this is what's going to happen here.

It's safe to assume that HTML pages know how to display themselves, so it makes sense to turn Display into a *display* method on the Login Page object. The result is that the Home Page calls that method by sending a message, containing a call action, to the Login Page. Figure 5-20 shows the objects and the message.

The third piece of the robustness diagram (Figure 5-6) contains the Customer, the Login Page, and the OK button on that page. In keeping with our current practice, we're going to represent the button in terms of a message to the Login Page. But first, we need to account for the Customer entering his or her user ID and password. Figure 5-21 shows the result.

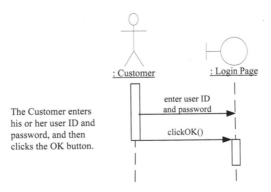

Figure 5-21: Log In Sequence Diagram, Part 3

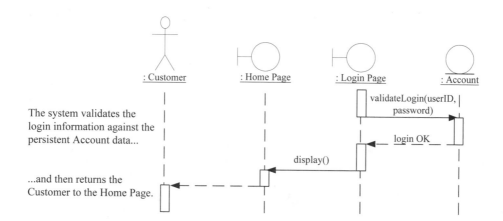

Figure 5-22: Log In Sequence Diagram, Part 4

If you're thinking that we need to show how the Login Page, which ended up with control in Figure 5-20, returns control to the Customer, you're right. The full sequence diagram, which appears toward the end of this section, addresses that need.

The fourth and final piece of our Log In robustness diagram (Figure 5-7) contains an actor (Customer), two boundary objects (the Home Page and the OK button), an entity object (Account), and two control objects (Validate Login Info and Display). As a result, the final piece of the sequence diagram we're building will be a little more complicated than the other three pieces.

Just as we assumed that an HTML page knows how to display itself, so we can assume that a persistent object knows how to check the values of its attributes. This means we can have our Account object perform the logic specified by the Validate Login Info control object from the robustness diagram. In contrast to the previous call actions we've seen, this time the user ID and the password, which the Customer entered, will appear as parameters in the message that calls the *validate* method on the Account.

Since we're only dealing with the basic course of action here, we only have a positive result of that method call, which is that there is an Account object that contains the specified user ID and password together. We show this result in the form of a return arrow from the Account back to the Login Page; let's go ahead and put a "Login OK" label on the message so it matches up with the robustness diagram.

Once the Login Page regains control, it needs to turn around and send a display yourself message back to the Home Page. At this point, we can show a return arrow going back to the Customer. Alternatively, we can omit that arrow with the understanding that even though the diagram appears to show that the Home Page is still in control, it's understood from the context that the system is waiting for the Customer to do something.

Figure 5-22 shows the last piece of our new sequence diagram. The figure splits the relevant use case sentence up to make it easier to see the correlation between the *what* of the use case and the *how* of the detailed design that the sequence diagram captures.

Figure 5-23 shows the full sequence diagram for the basic course of the Log In use case.

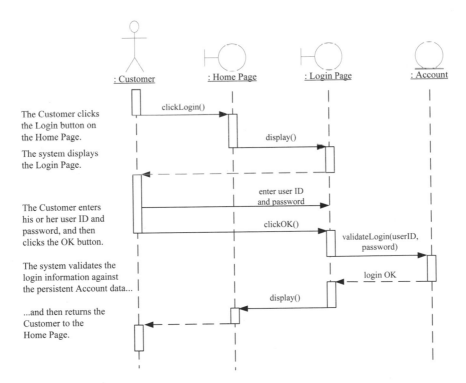

Figure 5-23: Final Log In Sequence Diagram

Collaboration Diagrams

The UML **collaboration diagram** is a diagram that focuses on the organization of the objects that participate in a given set of messages.

Collaboration diagrams are associated with the Design workflow (see Chapter 2) just as sequence diagrams are. As we'll see shortly, collaboration diagrams and sequence diagrams show the same information, so modelers are likely to use them at the same points of a development project.

Collaboration Diagram Notation

Collaboration diagrams show objects and messages, but not lifelines or focus-of-control rectangles, which only appear on sequence diagrams.

Generally speaking, the messages on a collaboration diagram have sequence numbers associated with them so you can read the messages in order. The UML standard is decimal numbering, which enables nesting. For instance, if one object sends a message to another object, which in turn sends a message to a third object, the messages would likely be numbered 1, 1.1, and 1.1.1, respectively.

Another useful feature of collaboration diagrams is the ability to show iteration easily. If an expression such as * [i = 1..n], or even just *, appears in front of a sequence number, it means that the given message is part of a loop. This can be awkward to show on a sequence diagram.

Figure 5-24 shows what the collaboration diagram might look like for the Log In use case.

As you can see, this collaboration diagram shows the same information as the sequence diagram shown in Figure 5-23. The difference is that the collaboration diagram focuses on the structural organization of the objects, whereas the sequence diagram focuses on the time ordering of the messages going back and forth among those objects. Whether you use one or both kinds of diagrams depends on your preference and what you're trying to model.

In case you're wondering, a robustness diagram is indeed a form of collaboration diagram without sequence numbers.

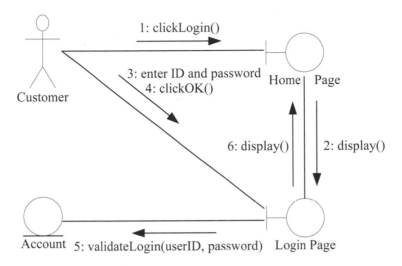

Figure 5-24: Collaboration Diagram

Expressing Time on Interaction Diagrams

Both sequence diagrams (by design) and collaboration diagrams (with the help of sequence numbers on messages) show what happens over time within a community of objects. The UML refers to both sequence diagrams and collaboration diagrams as **interaction diagrams**, because they show interactions among objects. It's often useful, though—especially when the system being modeled involves real-time operation or geographic distribution—to enhance interaction diagrams by specifying time-related requirements.

The UML defines the following time-specific terms:

- A **time expression** is an expression that resolves to a relative or absolute value of time once it's evaluated.

- A **timing mark** is a time-related name or label on a message.

- A **timing constraint** is a condition that must be satisfied with regard to time. A timing constraint usually contains a time expression; it may also contain a timing mark.

Figure 5-25: Timing on a Sequence Diagram

Figure 5-25 shows a timing constraint that might appear on the sequence diagram for the Log In use case.

The timing constraint in the figure uses a timing mark (*v*) and a time expression (*executionTime < 3 sec*). The presence of the timing mark on the message (*validateLogin*) makes it easier to refer to that message elsewhere on the sequence diagram (or its equivalent collaboration diagram).

You might also find timing constraints being used to model two special kinds of messages.

*   A **balking message** is like a synchronous message, except that the sending object gives up on the message if the receiving object is not ready to accept it. This might be represented using the timing constraint {wait = 0}.

*   A **timeout message** is also like a synchronous message, but in this case, the sender waits only for a specified period for the receiver to get ready to accept the message. The associated timing constraint might be something like {wait = 50 ms}.

Analysis Packages and Design Packages

Let's revisit the subject of packages, now that we have some more kinds of model elements to put in them.

The primary contents of the Unified Process analysis model are analysis classes, which were described at the beginning of this chapter. These classes are captured on robustness diagrams, so it makes sense to build on the idea of a package of classes and create an "analysis package" that contains analysis classes and the robustness diagrams that show their interactions.

See "Analysis" in Chapter 2 for more about the analysis model. See Figure 3-26 for examples of packages of classes.

Figure 5-26 shows what we'd have so far for an analysis package called Customer for our online bookstore.

Over time, the project team for The Internet Bookstore would expand this package to include robustness diagrams and analysis classes connected with use cases whose names would be the likes of Create Account and Change Billing Info. The original Shopping Cart package of use cases (see Figure 4-15) would get expanded into an analysis package, and so forth.

Sequence diagrams and collaboration diagrams belong to the design model (see Design in Chapter 2). Parallel to the analysis package is the concept of a "design package" that holds these diagrams. There should be obvious connections—*traceability*—between a design package and the analysis package whose contents provide the foundation for the design diagrams.

Figure 5-27 shows the beginnings of a design package for our bookstore.

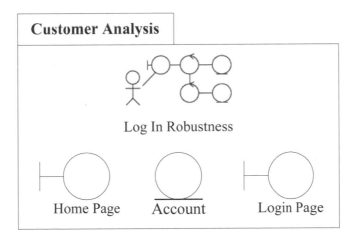

Figure 5-26: Sample Analysis Package

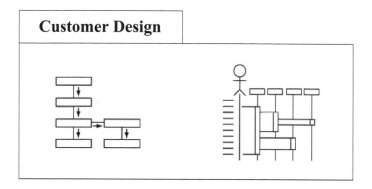

Figure 5-27: Sample Design Package

The design model also includes what the Unified Process calls "design classes," which are the subject of the next chapter.

Chapter 6

Refining the Structure of Things

Within the last two chapters, we looked at the various ways to model user and system behavior using the UML. Let's now switch back to the structural side of things, which we started looking at in Chapter 3, and see how a project team uses the UML to refine and expand the domain model for a system in response to the work they do in modeling behavior.

Abstract Classes

An **abstract class** is a class that can't have any instances.

Abstract classes are generally designed to capture operations that subclasses inherit. The idea is that the operations defined for an abstract class are relatively general, and each class that inherits these operations will refine and expand upon them.

 See "Generalization" in Chapter 3 for a discussion of inheritance.

Figure 6-1: Abstract Class Notation

In UML notation, the name of an abstract class appears in italics (see Figure 6-1).

Figure 6-2 shows the Review class, which was introduced in Chapter 3, as an abstract class.

Note that this diagram adds an abstract operation, *record*, to the Review class. Customer Review and Editorial Review will both inherit this operation, but the operation will work differently in the context of each class.

Dependencies

A **dependency** is a "using" relationship within which a change in one thing (such as a class) may affect another thing (for instance, another class).

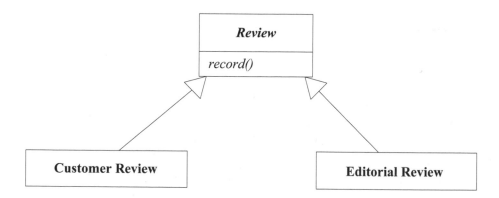

Figure 6-2: Sample Abstract Class

Figure 6-3: Dependency

We've already seen two examples of dependencies: the include and extend relationships involving use cases (see "Organizing Use Cases" in Chapter 4). The UML defines notation for a number of other types of dependencies, some of which are discussed later in this chapter.

You show a dependency involving two classes, which generally involves an operation of one class depending on another class, as a dashed line with a feathered arrow pointing at the independent class (see Figure 6-3).

Figure 6-4 shows a dependency that exists for our online bookstore. In this case, if the definition of the Book class changes, the way that the *checkAvailability* function works may have to change as well.

Attribute and Operation Details

The UML offers a variety of constructs that allow you to specify details for attributes and operations. These constructs are discussed in the following subsections.

Visibility

The concept of encapsulation was introduced in Chapter 3 (see "Objects"). The degree to which the elements of a class are encapsulated within that class depends on the level of visibility that's been assigned to them. The **visibility** of an attribute or an operation specifies whether objects that belong to other classes can "see" that attribute or operation.

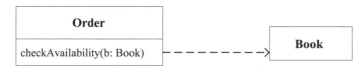

Figure 6-4: Sample Dependency

Figure 6-5: Visibility

The UML supports three levels of visibility.

- **Public visibility** (shown with a +) means that objects of any class can use the given attribute or operation.
- **Protected visibility** (#) means that only objects that belong to subclasses of the given class (at any level below that class) can use the attribute or operation.
- **Private visibility** (-) means that only objects belonging to the class itself can use the attribute or operation.

Figure 6-5 shows visibility adornments on attributes and operations that belong to our model for The Internet Bookstore.

The *assignRating* operation of the Customer Review class is public, which means that objects of any other class can use it. The *record* operation of Review is protected, so Customer Review objects and Editorial Review objects can use it, and objects of any subclasses of those two classes would be able to use it as well, but objects of classes outside that hierarchy won't be able to use *record*. The *emailAddress*, *ID*, and *password* attributes of Account are private: only Account objects have access to these. Similarly, Customer Review objects are the only ones that can use the *computeAvgRating* operation.

More about Attributes

The full form of a UML attribute declaration is this:

[*visibility*] *name* [*multiplicity*] [*: type*] [*= initial-value*] [*{property-string}*]

The rectangular brackets surround optional items, which means that only the name is required. However, UML diagrams will generally show details about attributes once serious design work commences on a project.

Visibility was discussed in the previous section, and examples of attribute types appeared in Chapter 3 (see Figure 3-3, for instance). An initial value of an attribute for a class means that each instance of that class (that is, each object that belongs to that class) will have that initial value for the given attribute.

The UML allows you to use the same multiplicity values that you use for associations (see Associations in Chapter 3). A multiplicity value on an attribute indicates how many instances of that attribute are present for each instance of the class. You put the multiplicity of an attribute between square brackets after the attribute name.

You can attach three properties to a UML attribute declaration.

- The *changeable* property indicates that you can change the value of the attribute, and you can also add other possible values. You might see this if you have a list of values that an attribute can assume. (If you don't specify a property for an attribute, it's assumed that the attribute is *changeable*.)

- The *addOnly* property indicates that you can add possible values for an attribute, but you can't change existing values.

- The *frozen* property indicates that you can't add or change possible values for an attribute. You'll generally see this property in the context of attributes that become unique identifiers.

Figure 6-6 shows details of some of the attributes that belong to one of the classes in our bookstore model.

An object belonging to the Account class can have between one and three email addresses. Each Account object has an ID that can't be deleted; you might think of this as being the equivalent of the key within a database table. And there's an initial value for an Account object's *password*, which the Customer is likely to change but which is useful in case the Customer forgets to define a password when he or she sets up an account.

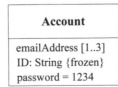

Figure 6-6: Attribute Details

More about Operations

The full form of a UML operation declaration is this:

[*visibility*] *name* [(*parameter-list*)] [: *returnType*] [{*property-string*}]

As with attributes, the rectangular brackets surround optional items.

A discussion of visibility appeared earlier in this chapter, and Chapter 3 included examples of operation return types (see Figure 3-6, for instance).

The parameters of an operation represent the data provided by the caller of the operation or the data that the operation returns to the caller, or both. The full form of a UML parameter declaration is this:

[*direction*] *name* : *type* [= *default-value*]

A parameter can have one of three directions:

- *in* (the operation can't modify the parameter, so the caller doesn't need to see it again)
- *out* (the operation sets or changes the value of the parameter and returns it to the caller)
- *inout* (the operation uses the value of the parameter and may also change the value; the caller expects to see an *inout* parameter again)

There are four properties that you can attach to a UML operation declaration.

- The *sequential* property indicates that only one call to a method within an instance of the given class can execute at a time. (Remember that what's called an "operation" for a class is referred to as a "method" for an object.)
- The *concurrent* property indicates that multiple calls to a method can execute simultaneously.
- The *guarded* property indicates that there can be multiple simultaneous calls to a method, but the object will execute only one call at a time.
- The *isQuery* property indicates that the operation doesn't change the values of any attributes.

The first three of these properties are relevant to the subject of threads, which are addressed in the next chapter. That chapter also talks about guard conditions, which are connected with the *guarded* property.

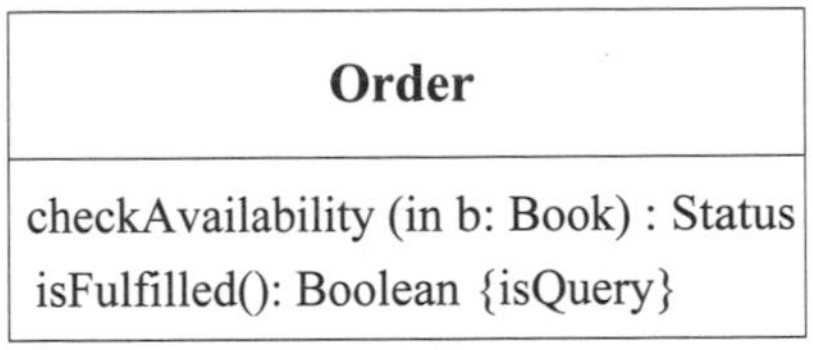

Order
checkAvailability (in b: Book) : Status isFulfilled(): Boolean {isQuery}

Figure 6-7: Operation Details

Figure 6-7 shows some details of operations belonging to our bookstore's Order class.

The *checkAvailability* operation receives a Book object (see Figure 3-3) and returns a value of the user-defined type Status. The *isFulfilled* operation is a query that returns True if everything the Customer ordered is in place, or False otherwise.

Extending the UML

The UML offers three kinds of ways to extend its basic notations for anything that might appear within a model: stereotypes, constraints, and tagged values.

Stereotypes

A **stereotype** is something that extends the basic vocabulary of the UML. You use stereotypes to build modeling constructs that aren't identified in the core UML, but are similar to things that are part of the core.

The UML defines more than 40 stereotypes that you can apply to things such as classes, associations, and packages. These add specific information that can be very useful to people who are working with the various UML diagrams. You can also define your own stereotypes; this comes in handy when you want to define kinds of model elements that are unique to your project.

Whether you use a UML-defined stereotype or one that you devise, you show the stereotype either as a name between guillemets (*«stereotypeName»*), in which case the stereotype appears as a label on the model element you're stereotyping, or as an icon of your choice.

Figure 6-8 shows some stereotypes relevant to The Internet Bookstore.

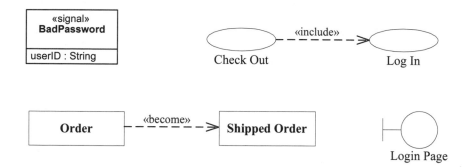

Figure 6-8: Stereotypes

All three of the labeled stereotypes are built into the UML. Signals were covered in Chapter 5 (see "Send"). The «become» stereotype indicates that an instance of Order "evolves into" an instance of a Shipped Order over time. The «include» stereotype was discussed in Chapter 4 (see "Organizing Use Cases").

Login Page has an icon as a stereotype; this is the symbol for a boundary object, which was introduced in Chapter 5. You can also represent the class to which a boundary object belongs as «boundary class». (Similarly, you show the other types of analysis classes as «entity class» and «control class». These three stereotypes are part of what's referred to as the Unified Process-Specific Extensions of the UML. The next version of the UML, 2.0, may include these as part of the mainstream.)

Constraints

A **constraint** is something that extends the semantics of an element of a model. You use a constraint to specify a condition that must hold true for an element of a model, such as an attribute or an association. For example, a constraint might specify the maximum execution time for a method, as shown in Chapter 5 (see Figure 5-25).

The UML defines about ten constraints, most of which apply to associations or generalizations. You can also define your own constraints.

You represent a constraint as a name or an expression between curly brackets (*{constraintName}* or *{expression})*) that appears near the constrained element.

Figure 6-9: Constraints

Figure 6-9 shows some constraints associated with our bookstore.

The {encrypted} constraint is user defined; it indicates that the passwords associated with Account objects must be encrypted in order to protect their integrity. The {or} and {ordered} constraints are defined within the UML. Within the figure, the former indicates that a Review can be either a Customer Review or an Editorial Review, and the latter indicates that the Reviews associated with a given Book must be dealt with in a particular order.

Tagged Values

A **tagged value** is something that extends the properties of a model element, but not instances of that element. For instance, a tagged value that applies to a class offers information about that class, but that information doesn't apply to objects that belong to that class.

The UML defines several tagged values, which apply to various kinds of model elements. You can also define your own tagged values.

You represent a tagged value as a pairing of a name and a value between curly brackets ({*tagName = value*}). You can also have just a value ({*tagValue*}).

Figure 6-10 shows some tagged values for our online bookstore.

Figure 6-10: Tagged Values

The tagged value on Editorial Review illustrates a common use of tagged values: to specify which future version of the system will contain a particular element. (There's a good chance that the project team will include things on diagrams and then decide to postpone further exploration of those things until future iterations.) The UML defines a tagged value called *persistence*; its allowable values include {transient} (which indicates that the given element has a relatively short life), and {persistent}. In the context of The Internet Bookstore, the results of a search are likely to be discarded once the Customer leaves the page that displays those results.

Interfaces and Classes

An **interface** is a collection of operations that represent services offered by a class or a component. (A discussion of components appears in Chapter 10.)

One of the key tenets of object orientation is the separation of an interface from the details of how the exposed operations are implemented. The interface specifies something like a contract that a class must adhere to; the class **realizes** (or provides a **realization** for) one or more interfaces.

The UML provides two ways to show an interface. One way is called "lollipop" notation; the interface is a circle attached to a class with a straight line. The other way involves defining the interface using a class box and the built-in «interface» stereotype, and drawing a dashed line with an open triangle at the end with the interface. See Figure 6-11 for an illustration of both kinds of notation.

Figure 6-12 shows two interfaces of interest to our online bookstore.

Setting up a Password Handler interface to the Account class provides the flexibility to use different encryption algorithms in the implementation of the operation that stores Customer passwords.

Figure 6-11: Class Interface Notation

Figure 6-12: Sample Class Interfaces

Along the same lines, the Inventory Handler interface allows elements of the system to interact with objects belonging to the Inventory class without having to know whether the inventory system uses FIFO (first in, first out), LIFO (last in, first out), or some other method of handling inventory.

We'll see interfaces in a different context in Chapter 10.

Template Classes

A **template class** is a construct that represents a family of potential classes. It has a set of formal parameters; you use the template to create a new class by binding a set of actual parameters to the template.

The concept of a template class comes more or less directly from C++. The Standard Template Library (STL) associated with that language makes heavy use of template classes.

The UML's longhand notation for a template class involves three elements.

- The box for the template class itself has a dashed-line rectangle in its upper right-hand corner that contains the formal parameters.

- The class to be bound to the template is shown with the usual class box, in any of its various forms.

- A dependency arrow (see Figure 6-3) points from the bound class to the template class; this arrow is labeled with the built-in «bind» stereotype. A list of the actual parameters sits next to the stereotype.

The shorthand notation is a class box with only one compartment, which contains the name of the bound class and a list of its actual parameters, separated by commas, within angle brackets.

Figure 6-13 shows both notations.

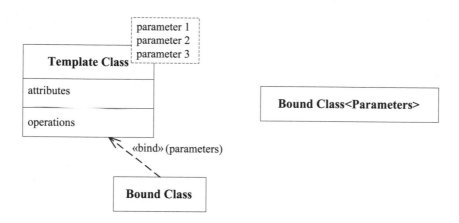

Figure 6-13: Template Class Notation

Figure 6-14 shows two ways to model a template class that might appear in a future release of The Internet Bookstore.

Cust Type and *Item Type* are the formal parameters for the Wish List template class; the «bind» dependency has the effect of creating a new Wish List class that accepts Holiday customers (those who only make purchases at holiday time) of CDs (as opposed to books). The notation on the right is shorthand for the same binding.

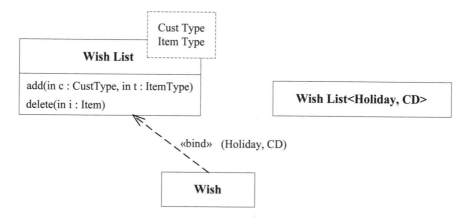

Figure 6-14: Sample Template Class

Design Classes and Packages

A development team typically starts defining classes at a relatively high level of abstraction, using only the kinds of notation described in Chapter 3. When the team starts doing preliminary design, the classes become more specific; if this activity takes the form of robustness analysis, we call the results analysis classes (see Robustness Analysis in Chapter 5). As the level of detail rises for the classes, as expressed by the various kinds of notation described in this chapter, they become what the Unified Process calls **design classes**.

Since in Chapter 5 we saw that an analysis package contains analysis classes, it's logical that a design package should contain design classes. As you might expect, design classes belong to the design model (see Chapter 2), which is basically a package of design packages.

Figure 6-15 expands upon the design package of Figure 5-27 by including design classes that appear on the sequence diagram for the Log In use case (see Figure 5-23).

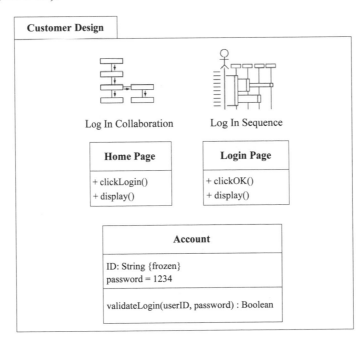

Figure 6-15: Sample Design Package

Note that the class boxes in this package show operations that belong to the various classes. The operation for Account didn't appear in the original class diagrams in Chapter 3, and we didn't show operations for the "page" classes in Chapter 5. This is an example of how the building of the structure of a system is driven by the exploration of the required behavior of that system. A use case leads to a sequence diagram that the team uses to allocate behavior among the objects mentioned in the use cases. This behavior takes the form of methods, which in turn become operations on the classes to which those objects belong. The phrase "use case driven," then, truly comes to life.

Over the next three chapters, we'll look at various other kinds of elements that belong in the design model.

Chapter 7

Describing Flows

Let's now move back into the arena of dynamic behavior. This chapter looks at how we can use the UML to model the details of the work that objects do, both internally and in conjunction with other objects, and also to model the details of computational processes.

Activities and Actions

An **activity** is something that an object performs on an ongoing basis. An activity is nonatomic, which means it can be interrupted. You can also decompose an activity into other activities.

As discussed in Chapter 5 (see Messages and Actions), an **action** is a set of executable computations that results in changes to the values of one or more attributes or the return of a value to some object, or both. Unlike an activity, an action is atomic—it can't be interrupted. You might think of an action as an activity that can't be decomposed.

It's assumed that an activity lasts for some duration, whereas an action takes an insignificant amount of time, relatively speaking.

The UML notation is the same for an activity and an action: a lozenge (in other words, a symbol with long, straight lines on top and bottom and short sides that are curved outward), as you can see in Figure 7-1.

Figure 7-1: Activity/Action Notation

Figure 7-2 shows some activities and actions associated with The Internet Bookstore.

The differences between activities and actions should generally be obvious from the context. Figure 7-2 shows two actions that are each made up of one expression, and three activities that each involve several different kinds of actions.

An object will generally perform some activities and actions sequentially. Often, of course, there will be divergent paths. Divergence is the subject of the next two sections.

Branching and Merging

A **branch** is a decision point at which there are two or more possible paths of flow of control. A **merge** is a point at which two or more branched paths come together.

The UML represents both a branch and a merge with a diamond shape (see Figure 7-3).

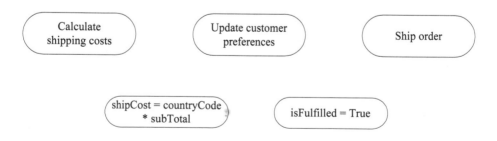

Figure 7-2: Sample Activities and Actions

Figure 7-3: Branch/Merge Notation

This symbol is, indeed, basically the same symbol that appears on the trusty flowchart. The only real difference is that standard flowchart notation doesn't show merges with diamonds; flows generally come back together between activities on a flowchart (in other words, on the arrows between activities or actions).

Each possible path out of a branch has a **guard condition**. This is a Boolean expression that must evaluate to True in order for the branch to be taken. The collection of all paths out of a branch must cover all of the possibilities; you might see the word "else" on one path to account for "none of the above." The guard conditions can't overlap with each other, though.

You show a guard condition within square brackets near a path out of a branch, as you can see in Figure 7-4, which depicts some branching and merging that will occur within our bookstore.

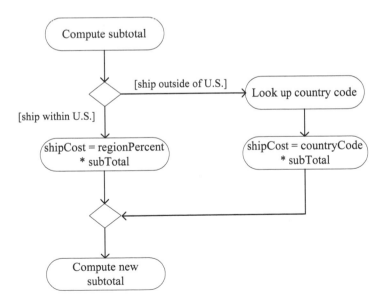

Figure 7-4: Sample Branching and Merging

The first activity that the Order performs is to compute the initial subtotal. This is probably the total of the costs of the books contained within the Order (see Figure 3-14). Then a branch occurs because the Order computes the shipping cost for itself differently based on where the Customer wants it shipped. Once that cost has been calculated, the divergent paths merge, and the Order performs the action of adding the cost to the running subtotal.

The arrows that come into and go out of activities show what the UML calls **transitions**. These show how the flow of control passes between activities or actions. Transitions are discussed later in this chapter and also in Chapter 8.

Forking and Joining

A **fork** is a splitting of a flow of control into two or more flows of control, each of which operates independent of, and concurrent with, the others. A **join** is a synchronization of two or more flows of control into one flow.

Forks and joins are particularly useful in modeling processes and threads, which are discussed at the end of this chapter.

The symbol that represents both forks and joins is a long, thin, black rectangle called a **synchronization bar** (see Figure 7-5).

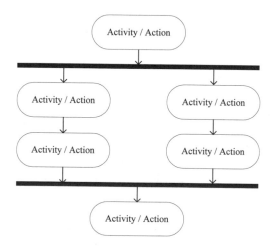

Figure 7-5: Fork and Join Notation

The fork occurs after the first activity/action is complete. The activities/ actions on the parallel paths might involve separate methods, or they might involve some of the same methods if the associated operations on the object's class have been labeled with the *concurrent* property (see "More about Operations" in Chapter 6). Once all of the parallel activities/actions have finished, a join occurs, and the object resumes strictly sequential processing.

Figure 7-6 shows forking and joining that occurs in connection with a bookstore Order.

Once the system has received an Order, it can perform the first three activities after the fork in parallel, because they operate within separate parts of the system. The system proceeds with the shipping activity once the activities along each divergent path are complete.

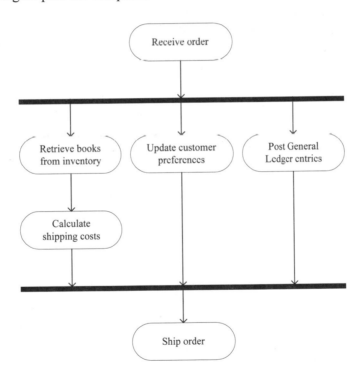

Figure 7-6: Sample Forking and Joining

Activity Diagrams

An **activity diagram** shows the flows among activities associated with a given object, including transitions, branches and merges, and forks and joins.

You'll generally see activity diagrams in two contexts: modeling some kind of workflow, and describing the workings of some algorithm or detailed computation.

Figure 7-7 shows part of an activity diagram relevant to our bookstore. The black circle at the top of the diagram represents the "initial state." The concentric circles at the bottom represent the "final state." These terms are defined in the next chapter.

Note that on an activity diagram, the transitions are "triggerless," which means that they happen unconditionally. In Chapter 8, we'll look at other kinds of transitions.

Swimlanes

You can group activities and actions on an activity diagram with the help of vertical lines. Each pair of lines delineates what's called a **swimlane**, which is simply a lane down which you can track activities and actions associated with, for instance, a particular part of an organization.

Figure 7-8 shows swimlanes that might be associated with the partial activity diagram from Figure 7-7.

The complete activity diagram for our Order object would show plenty of communication across swimlanes. The boundaries are strictly conceptual.

Object Flow

You can enhance an activity diagram with **object flows**, which are simply dependencies that show the details of how the object(s) involved in the various activities/actions are specifically affected.

The UML provides two ways to show objects within object flows. The first way involves showing the new values for one or more attributes, using the standard attribute notation (*attribute = value*). The second way involves showing a "state" value in square brackets ([*state*]).

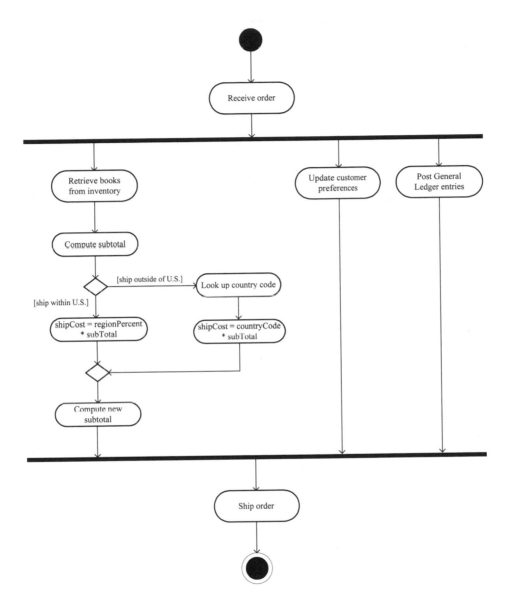

Figure 7-7: Sample Activity Diagram

Object state is the subject of the next chapter; in the meantime, you can think of the state of an object as being the collection of the values of its attributes at a given point in time.

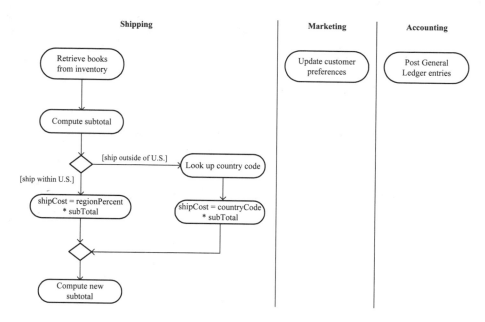

Figure 7-8: Swimlanes

Figure 7-9 shows examples of both notations as they apply to some of the changes that an Order object goes through within our bookstore system.

The diagram implies that an Order's *prefsRecorded* attribute has False as its initial value when the Order gets created. It's good practice to make this explicit on whatever class diagrams show the Order class. The diagram also implies that an Order object has an attribute called something like *hasBeen-Posted*, which starts off False and is set to True when the General Ledger posting activity is complete.

Processes, Threads, and Active Objects

A **process** is a heavyweight flow of control. Generally, a program running under an operating system such as Windows or UNIX lives within a process, and each process has some kind of unique identifier. A **thread** is a lightweight flow of control that generally runs inside a process.

An **active object** is an object that can own a process or a thread. An **active class**, therefore, is a class whose instances are active objects.

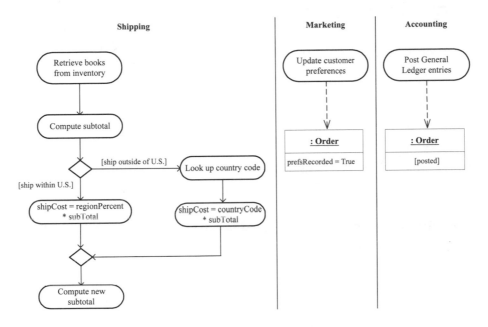

Figure 7-9: Object Flows

You differentiate an active class from a passive object, or an active object from a passive object, by making the border around the class box or object box thicker than usual for the active entity. Figure 7-10 shows our bookstore's Order class as an active class, and an instance of Order as an active object.

In the context of our online bookstore, it's likely that each Order object controls a process, and that each of the various paths that appear on the full activity diagram (of which Figure 7-7 is an excerpt) probably represents a thread that has an associated active object. You can use two stereotypes built into the UML to label active classes and active objects as processes and threads, as shown in Figure 7-11.

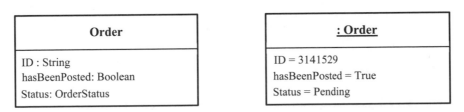

Figure 7-10: Sample Active Class and Active Object

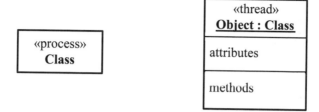

Figure 7-11: Process and Thread Stereotypes

Activity Diagrams and Packages

Since activity diagrams tend to contain design-level details, it makes sense to put them into design packages. Figure 7-12 shows what one of the design packages might look like for the Order-related materials for our bookstore.

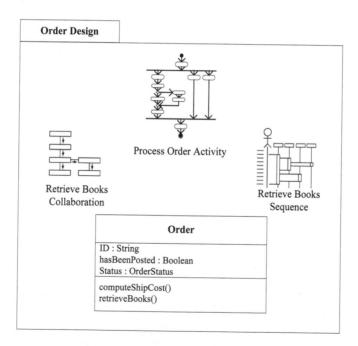

Figure 7-12: Design Package with Activity Diagram

Chapter 8

Tracking the Lives of Things

Let's continue to explore the inner workings of individual objects. This chapter looks at the things that an object goes through while it's "alive" within a system.

Events

An **event** is an occurrence of interest to an object.

The UML supports the representation of four kinds of events.

- A **signal** is an asynchronous communication between objects.
- A **call event** is a synchronous communication that involves an object invoking a method on another object or an object invoking one of its own methods on itself. A call event is basically equivalent to a call action.
- A **time event** is an event that occurs after a specified period of time. You express a time event using the word "after" followed by a time expression. For instance, you might see *after 5 seconds* or *after (15 minutes since last keyboard or mouse action)*.

- A **change event** is an event that occurs when some condition is satisfied. You express a change event using the word "when" followed by a Boolean expression. For example, you might see *when midnight* or *when maximumLoops = 100*.

 See Send in Chapter 5 for more about signals, Figure 5-25 for more about time expressions, and "Call and Return," also in Chapter 5, for more about call actions.

How an object responds to a particular event depends, in part, on the state that object is in when it receives the event.

States, Transitions, and Guard Conditions

The following subsections describe the various conditions in which an object can reside, and how an object moves from one condition to another.

States

A **state** is a condition in which an object can be at some point during its lifetime, for some finite amount of time.

An object can do any or all of the following while it's in a particular state:

- Perform an activity (see Activities and Actions in Chapter 7)
- Wait for an event (see the previous section)
- Satisfy one or more conditions

The UML notation for a state is a rectangle with rounded corners, as shown in Figure 8-1.

State

Figure 8-1: State Notation

Figure 8-2: Sample States

Figure 8-2 shows some states that an Order object can assume within our online bookstore.

When an Order is in the Posting state, it performs an activity that involves other objects—in this case, objects that belong to the Accounting portion of the system. (It's fairly common for other objects to be involved with a given object's activities.) The Shipped state is an example of a state in which an object has satisfied some condition. We'll see the Retrieving Books state again in several places later in this chapter.

Transitions

A **transition** is a change of an object from one state (the **source state**) to another (the **target state**).

A transition "fires" when an event (see page 99) of interest to the given object occurs. (The event "triggers" the transition.) Alternatively, a transition may fire unconditionally when the object is ready to move from one state to another, generally because the activity associated with the source state is complete. This is called a **triggerless transition**. Figure 8-3 shows the UML notations for a triggered transition (top) and a triggerless transition (bottom).

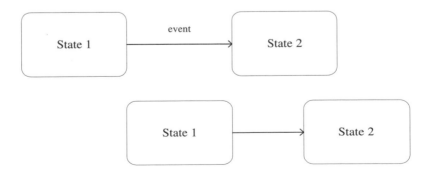

Figure 8-3: Transition Notation

Figure 8-4: Transition with Action

There may be an action associated with a triggered transition. Unless there's also a guard condition (discussed in the next subsection), this action executes unconditionally before the object enters the target state. Figure 8-4 shows the notation for a transition with an associated action.

An object doesn't have to go from one state to a different state within a transition. A **self-transition** is a transition whose source state and target state are the same. (We'll see why such a thing exists later in the chapter, when we look at "internal" transitions.) Figure 8-5 shows how you represent a self-transition using the UML.

Figure 8-6 shows some transitions that an Order object might make in the context of The Internet Bookstore.

The transition from Packaging to Shipping is triggerless, just like the ones that appear on activity diagrams (see Chapter 7). The transition from Shipping to Shipped occurs when the *shipConfirm* event occurs; the Order object records the change in state by performing a call action (invoking the *setFulfilledFlag* method on itself). The Retrieving Books state has a self-transition.

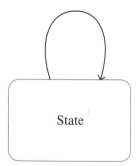

Figure 8-5: Self-Transition

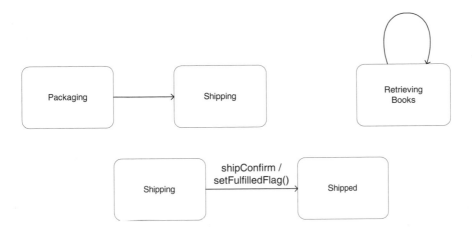

Figure 8-6: Sample Transitions

Guard Conditions

A **guard condition**, in this context, is a Boolean expression that must evaluate to True before a given transition can fire.

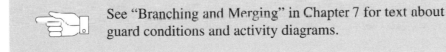

See "Branching and Merging" in Chapter 7 for text about guard conditions and activity diagrams.

You show a guard condition in square brackets near the transition arrow.

- If a guard condition is associated with an event, you use the form

    eventName [guard condition]

    If the Boolean evaluates to False, the object ignores the event and does not change states.

- If you have an event, a guard condition, and an action, the form is

    eventName [guard condition] / action

    Again, if the Boolean is False, the object doesn't execute the action, and no state change occurs.

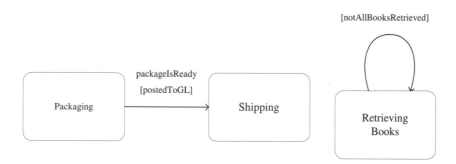

Figure 8-7: Guard Conditions

- You can also have a guard condition by itself on a transition, which takes the form

[guard condition]

Figure 8-7 shows some guard conditions that might apply to transitions associated with an Order object.

The transition between Packaging and Shipping occurs when the *packageIs-Ready* event comes in *and* it's been established that the associated Order has been posted to the General Ledger (GL). The Order object stays in the Retrieving Books state until the Order realizes that it's accumulated all of the books that the Customer requested.

State Machines and Statechart Diagrams

State machine is a fancy term for the combination of the following:

- The states that an object can assume during its life
- The events to which that object can respond
- The possible responses the object can make to those events
- The transitions that occur between the object's states.

A UML **statechart diagram** (also known as a **state diagram**) shows an object's state machine.

Figure 8-8 shows part of a statechart diagram for our online bookstore's Order object.

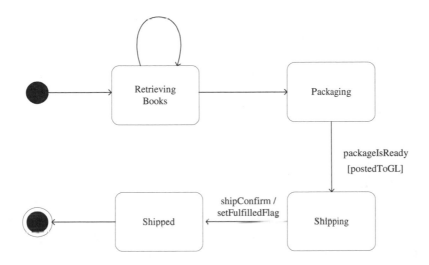

Figure 8-8: Statechart (State) Diagram

This diagram includes two symbols introduced in the previous chapter (see Figure 7-7).

- The solid black circle represents the **initial state**, which is the starting point of the state machine for an object.

- The solid circle and open circle pair represents the **final state**, which is the stopping point for the state machine.

Neither an initial state nor a final state is considered a full state: each can have a name, but none of the other aspects of states described in the next section. Also, you may see a statechart diagram without a final state, which means that the object has, in effect, perpetual life.

More about States and Transitions

On a state diagram, the symbol for a state may contain any of several other pieces of information.

- An **entry action** is an action that the object always performs immediately upon entering the given state. This appears as *entry / actionName* within the state symbol. If a self-transition occurs, the object performs the entry action.

- An **exit action**, similarly, is an action that the object always performs immediately before leaving the given state, in response to a regular transition or a self-transition. This appears in the form *exit / actionName*.

- In many cases, an object doesn't do anything except wait while it's in a particular state. However, you can show, within the state symbol, an activity that the object performs while it's in the state, using the notation *do / activityName*. Remember that an activity is interruptible, which means that when an event comes in, the object is likely to stop performing the activity and respond to the event.

- An object may handle reception of an event by performing some action while remaining in the existing state. This is called an **internal transition**; it's shown as *eventName / actionName*. If an object makes an internal transition, it does *not* execute the exit action or the entry action. (Note how this is different from a self-transition, which *does* result in the execution of the exit action and then the entry action.)

- A **deferred event** is an event that's of interest to the object, but which the object defers handling until the object reaches a different state. This is shown as *eventName / defer*. Deferred events get put into a queue; when the object changes state, the first thing that the object does is check to see whether there are events in the queue to which it can now respond.

Composite States

The states we've looked at so far have all been what the UML calls simple states. Now let's look at the key aspects of **composite states**, which are states that can have multiple nested states, or **substates**.

Sequential Substates

If an object can be in a composite state and only one of that state's substates at the same time, the substates are referred to as **sequential substates**. There are transitions between the substates just as there would be transitions between full states.

Figure 8-9 shows the UML notation for a composite state composed of sequential substates.

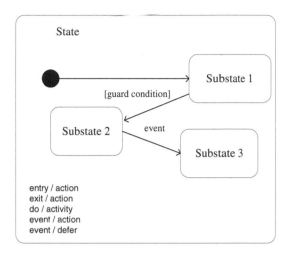

Figure 8-9: Composite State with Sequential Substates

Figure 8-10 shows some of the sequential substates that make up the Retrieving Books state that's been appearing in this chapter's diagrams.

When an Order object enters the Retrieving Books state, it also enters the Accumulating from Inventory substate.

If the system is able to retrieve all of the books for the Order from inventory, the object leaves the Accumulating from Inventory substate *and* the Retrieving Books state and enters the Packaging state. On the other hand, if there are any books on back order, the Order enters the Waiting for Back Order substate, where it remains until the back-ordered books arrive.

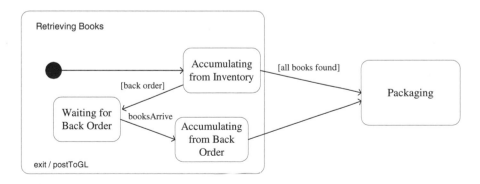

Figure 8-10: Sample Sequential Substates

At that point, the object enters the Accumulating from Back Order state, and at some point the object leaves that substate and the enclosing state and enters the Packaging state. Regardless of what substate the object is in when it leaves the Retrieving Books state, though, the last thing that happens is execution of the *postToGL* exit action.

Here are some more interesting tidbits about substates:

- A substate within a composite state can have any or all of the details that can be associated with a regular state, such as entry actions, activities, and deferred events (see More about States and Transitions).

- A source state, which resides outside a given composite state, can have an associated transition whose target state is either the composite state as a whole or any one of the substates that compose that state. (If the target of the transition is the composite state itself, you start with the initial state symbol in tracing the flow.)

- Similarly, a transition can come out of a substate and then leave the enclosing composite state without having to go through the other sub-states.

History State

As mentioned in the previous subsection, it's assumed that when an object makes a transition to a composite state, the flow starts with the initial state within that state. However, you can use a **history state** to "remember" the last substate that the object was in before it left the composite state. This means that an event can interrupt an activity, but then the object can pick up where it left off once it's handled that event.

Figure 8-11 shows how we associate a history state—represented by an H within a small circle—with our Retrieving Books composite state.

When a *query* event comes in while an Order object is in the Retrieving Books state, the system puts the current activity on hold and puts the object in the Checking Status state. When the activities associated with that state are finished, the system puts the Order back into the Retrieving Books state and the substate in which the Order resided when activity was interrupted, and the Order resumes performing the interrupted activity.

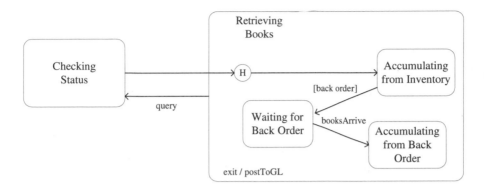

Figure 8-11: History State

Concurrent Substates

If an object can be in a composite state but can also be in more than one of that state's substates at the same time, the substates are referred to as **concurrent substates**.

In this situation, two or more sets of substates can represent parallel flows of control. When the object enters a composite state with concurrent substates, the object also enters the initial states of each set of substates. Just like on an activity diagram, you can resynchronize these parallel flows. On a state diagram, however, you show this resynchronization by using a final state for each parallel set of concurrent substates.

Figure 8-12 shows how we use the UML to represent some concurrent substates that belong to the Shipping state, another one of the states in which our Order object can reside.

When an Order object enters the Shipping state, it also enters the Filling Out Shipping Slip substate and the Posting Final Amount to GL substate at the same time. Work proceeds along both paths in parallel; there aren't any dependencies between the activities associated with the path labeled Physical and those in the path labeled Financial. Once the Order reaches the final states along both paths, the object leaves the Shipping state.

Transitions in and out of composite states with concurrent substates work the same way as they do for states with sequential substates. You can also use a history state in conjunction with concurrent substates.

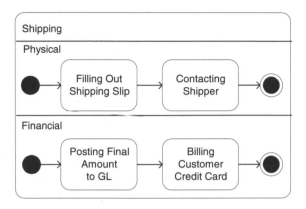

Figure 8-12: Concurrent Substates

State Diagrams and Packages

Because development teams tend to draw state diagrams during detailed design, their logical destination is design packages. Figure 8-13 shows an updated version of the package presented in Figure 7-12.

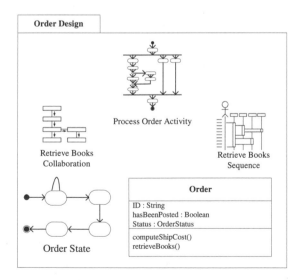

Figure 8-13: Design Package with State Diagram

Chapter 9

Showing How Groups of Things Work Together

Let's move away from the examination of specific objects and back to groups of objects.

Collaborations

A **collaboration** is a collection of classes, interfaces, and other elements that work together to provide some behavior.

You can think of a collaboration as being a conceptual chunk of a system. It's at the collaboration level that the models for a system really start getting fleshed out, and people can see how things are coming together.

The UML notation for a collaboration is similar to that for a use case (see Figure 4-3), except that a collaboration appears as an ellipse with a dashed outline, rather than the solid outline of a use case. Figure 9-1 shows two of the collaborations present within the model for The Internet Bookstore.

Figure 9-1: Collaborations

A collaboration has a structural part and a behavioral part.

You'll generally see the structure of a collaboration shown on a class diagram. The elements of a collaboration can participate in the same kinds of relationships that appear on a class diagram, such as associations and dependencies. One key difference is that collaborations tend to include elements that cut across different levels of a system, whereas a typical class diagram shows classes and interfaces for only one level.

See Figure 3-20 in Chapter 3 for an example of a class diagram.

Collaboration diagrams (as you might expect) and sequence diagrams (see Chapter 5) capture the behavioral aspects of a collaboration. Both types of diagrams show the interactions among various objects to accomplish some purpose.

A **realization** involving a collaboration is a relationship between that collaboration and a use case or an operation. (We'll look at another type of realization in the next chapter.) A realization represents a move from a high-level abstraction to something more concrete.

As mentioned in Chapter 5, a robustness diagram is another form of collaboration diagram. According to the Unified Process, a robustness diagram shows what's called a **use case realization—analysis**. This is a collaboration, belonging to the analysis model (see "Analysis" in Chapter 2), that describes how a use case is realized and performed in terms of analysis objects.

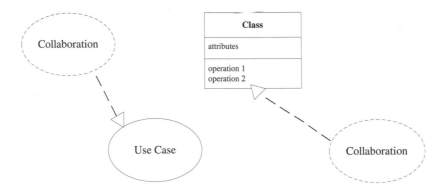

Figure 9-2: Realization Notation

You show a realization with a dashed line from the collaboration to the thing it realizes, and an open triangle, like the one used for generalization (see Figure 3-15), at the end where the realized thing lies. See Figure 9-2.

Figure 9-3 shows realizations associated with the collaborations that appear in Figure 9-1.

We show a collaboration realizing the Modify Order use case, and a collaboration for the *computeShippingCost* operation, because the use case and the operation both call upon several different classes. Shipping costs were discussed in Chapter 7 (see Figure 7-4, for instance); we'll look at order modification again later in this chapter.

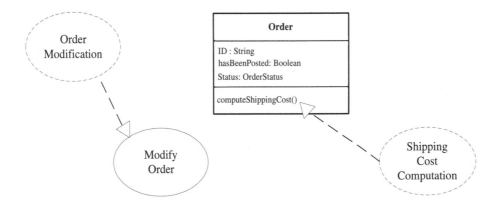

Figure 9-3: Sample Realizations

Patterns, Mechanisms, and Frameworks

The following subsections describe three types of UML constructs that reside at the next level of abstraction above collaborations.

Patterns

The UML defines a **pattern** as a solution to a problem that's common to a variety of contexts.

Books have been written about several kinds of patterns, including the following:

- Analysis patterns (such as Observation, which can be used to measure the values of qualitative attributes)
- Business patterns (for instance, an Employment pattern describes a contract between employer and employee)
- Organizational patterns (examples include patterns associated with continuous improvement)
- Process patterns (for example, Time-To-Customer, which has associated processes designed to shorten the time it takes to fulfill a customer order)

Of primary interest to our exploration of patterns are design patterns and architectural patterns, which are the subjects of the next two subsections.

Mechanisms

A **design pattern** is a pattern that comes into play during the design phase of a software development project. Design patterns are generally easy to understand and highly reusable across projects. In UML terms, a **mechanism** is a design pattern that applies to a society of classes.

A mechanism takes one of two forms. The first form is a simple collaboration. The second form is a **parameterized collaboration**. The basic idea is similar to that behind the template class, except that a parameterized collaboration has roles as its formal parameters, instead of attributes or data types.

Figure 9-4 shows how the UML represents a parameterized collaboration.

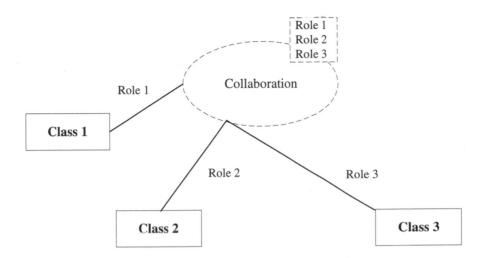

Figure 9-4: Parameterized Collaboration

 See "Template Classes" in Chapter 6 for more about template classes. See Figure 3-9 for more about roles.

The Proxy design pattern is widely used in the design of systems that keep strict separation between interfaces and implementations. Figure 9-5 shows how The Internet Bookstore makes use of this pattern in the context of a Customer and an Order that he or she has placed.

As with a template class, the formal parameters of a design pattern appear in a box in the upper right corner of the collaboration ellipse. In this case:

- Our bookstore's Customer is the Client.

- When that Customer interacts with the system in connection with an order, he or she will do so via a general-purpose Order Interface.

- The Customer will actually work with an Order Proxy, because the real Order has a number of different aspects that will be distributed across various classes and, most likely, across different pieces of hardware as well. We'll explore the distribution of software in the next chapter.

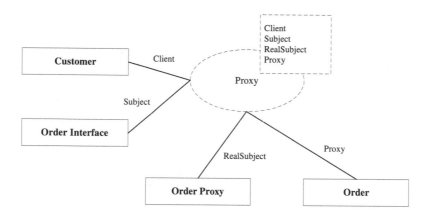

Figure 9-5: Proxy Pattern

Let's take a look underneath the hood of this mechanism.

Figure 9-6 shows the structural aspects of our version of the Proxy pattern.

This diagram adds a *modify* operation, which is connected with the Modify Order use case introduced in Figure 9-3. This operation is defined as abstract within the Order Interface class because Order Proxy and Order, both of which inherit the operation, actually define how the operation works. In this case, the Order Proxy version of *modify* simply calls the Order version of the operation, as indicated by the note attached to Order Proxy. The *realOrder* role on the association between Order Proxy and Order completes the static representation of the Proxy design pattern.

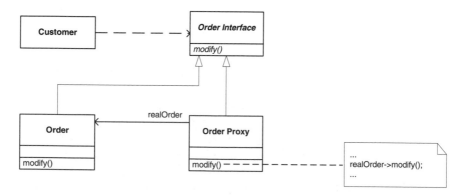

Figure 9-6: Proxy Pattern Structure

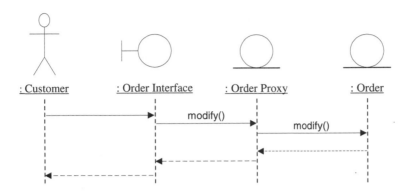

Figure 9-7: Proxy Pattern Behavior

Figure 9-7 shows the behavioral aspects of Proxy as it applies to an Order for our bookstore.

The Customer performs his or her part of the Modify Order use case using the Order Interface. When he or she is ready to commit modifications, the Order Interface calls *modify* on the appropriate Order Proxy object, which in turn calls *modify* on the associated Order object. When the Order has finished modifying itself, control eventually finds its way back to the Customer.

By setting things up this way, the project team for The Internet Bookstore builds in the ability to change how an Order gets modified without having to change the Order Interface.

Frameworks

The UML defines a **framework** as an architectural pattern that provides a template that you can use to extend applications.

It's useful to think of a framework as being a mini-architecture that contains mechanisms. You can include simple collaborations, parameterized collaborations, or both within a framework. Ultimately, the full framework for a system forms the system's complete architecture.

One widely used framework is the Model-View-Controller (MVC) architectural pattern, which comes from the Smalltalk language. The guiding principle is that you use this framework to separate the basic objects (the Model) from their presentation (the View) and the things that keep those two in synch (the Controller).

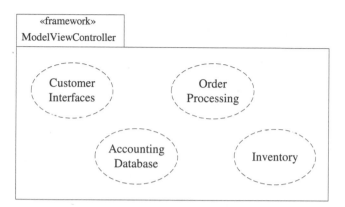

Figure 9-8: Model-View-Controller Pattern

It's no coincidence that this pattern offers a strong correlation with robustness analysis notation (see Chapter 5): Model represents entity objects, View represents boundary objects, and Controller represents control objects.

The UML notation for a framework is a stereotyped package of collaborations. Figure 9-8 shows how we use the UML to represent the MVC pattern using some of the key architectural features of our online bookstore.

The Accounting Database collaboration, which represents persistently stored data, lives on the Model level, Customer Interfaces lives on the View level, and Order Processing and Inventory live on the Controller level. Of course, a complete view of the framework for our online bookstore would include a number of other collaborations on each of these levels.

Systems and Subsystems

In UML terms, a **system** is a stereotyped package that contains all of the models that the project team produces along the way.

By extension, a **subsystem** is a grouping of related elements that is part of a system. You also show a subsystem as a stereotyped package. As a package, a subsystem owns a set of elements contained within different models: an element can be part of only one subsystem. Thus, the UML notion of a subsystem gives the project team an easy way to partition the pieces of the system. The system package, in turn, owns all of the subsystems.

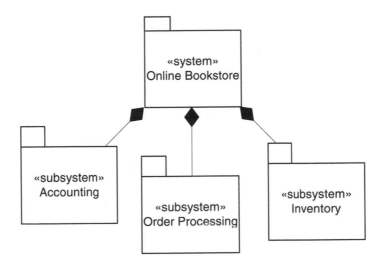

Figure 9-9: Systems and Subsystems

Figure 9-9 shows how we represent some of our bookstore's subsystems, and the system as a whole, using the UML.

Systems "roll up" subsystems using composition relationships. **Composition** is a strong form of aggregation (see Chapter 3) within which the "parts" live and die with the "whole." In other words, a subsystem can't exist except as part of a system.

In the next, and last, chapter, we'll look at those aspects of the UML that are used in modeling the tangible pieces of systems.

Chapter 10

Describing How Things Will Be Built

Let's conclude our exploration of the UML with a look at the diagrams that show how the various pieces of a system come together in the real world.

Components

A **component** is a physical and replaceable part of a system that conforms to, and realizes, a set of interfaces.

Components are one of two grouping mechanisms in the UML. The other mechanism is the package, which was introduced in Chapter 3 and talked about in other chapters as well. Whereas a package is a *conceptual* grouping of elements of a model, though, a component is a *physical* grouping of elements.

A component's interfaces are comparable to the interfaces associated with classes (see "Interfaces and Classes" in Chapter 6). For instance, a component *realizes* interfaces, as does a class.

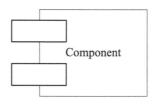

Figure 10-1: UML Component Notation

There are some important differences between components and classes, though:

• A component is a *physical* thing that lives on some piece of hardware; a class is *conceptual*.

• Something talking to a component can generally only access the operations it encompasses through its interfaces, and that thing can't access a component's attributes directly at all. A class can expose its attributes to subclasses (this is *protected* visibility; see Chapter 6) or to everyone (this is *public* visibility).

The UML notation for a component is a large rectangle with two smaller rectangles serving as tabs on its left-hand side (see Figure 10-1).

The two notations for the relationships between components and interfaces are the same as those for classes and interfaces. "Lollipop" notation shows the interface as a circle attached to a component with a straight line. The other notation involves defining the interface as a stereotyped class and drawing a dashed line from the component to the interface, with an open triangle at the end with the interface. See Figure 10-2 for illustrations of both methods of notation for component interfaces.

Figure 10-3 shows both notations for a component and a related interface that belong to The Internet Bookstore.

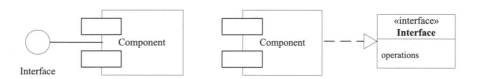

Figure 10-2: Components and Interfaces

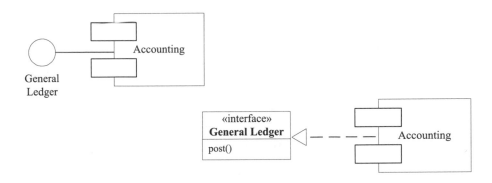

Figure 10-3: Sample Component and Component Interface

The Accounting component realizes the General Ledger interface. Components that wish to post to the General Ledger (GL), which is part of Accounting, can only do so via the interface.

The UML assigns components to one of three categories.

- A **deployment component** is an executable part of a system. The UML defines two stereotypes for use on deployment components: *«executable»*, which usually indicates a binary (EXE) file, and *«library»*, which indicates a static or dynamic object library such as a dynamic link library (DLL).

- A **work product component** is a component that's part of the system but isn't executable. There are three UML-defined stereotypes for work product components: *«table»* (for a database table), *«file»* (for a file that contains source code), and *«document»*.

- An **execution component** is created as a result of an executing system. One kind of execution component is a COM+ object, which a system creates as an instantiation of a DLL at runtime.

You can represent a component by using either the UML standard notation, as shown in Figure 10-1, or as an icon. Figure 10-4 shows some other components of our online bookstore, using iconic stereotypes.

The figure shows icons that represent UML-defined stereotypes for three kinds of components: a «table» (GLAccount.tbl, which holds General Ledger accounts), an «executable» (GL.exe, which is the main executable program associated with the General Ledger), and a «file» (GLAccount.h, which contains source code associated with the GLAccount table).

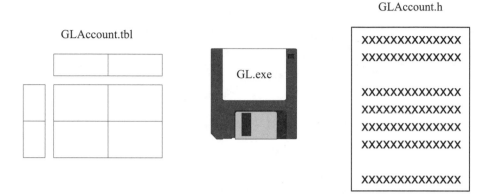

Figure 10-4: Components as Iconic Stereotypes

Component Diagrams

A **component diagram** shows a collection of related components.

You might think of a component diagram as a type of class diagram that shows components instead of classes. This kind of diagram can show the various kinds of relationships that components can have, which are the same as the ones classes can have. Generally, though, the focus will be on the interfaces that components expose and use, and the dependencies that exist among the various components. (Dependency arrows on a component diagram show how each component uses interfaces exposed by other components.)

Figure 10-5 shows a component diagram for our bookstore that uses the standard UML notation for components, with label stereotypes.

This diagram shows the key components associated with a Customer search. First, the Customer moves from the front (home) page to the Search page. When he or she has defined some search criteria and asked the system to proceed, the search program takes over. The program will search on the Book table or the Author table, or both, depending on the criteria specified by the Customer.

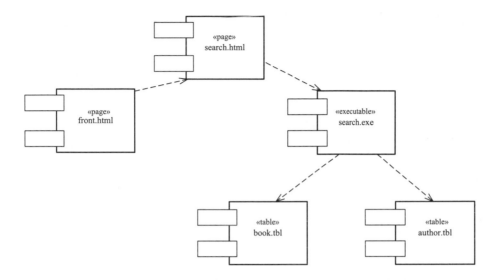

Figure 10-5: Component Diagram with Label Stereotypes

Figure 10-6 is a component diagram that shows other aspects of the model for our bookstore, using stereotype icons. The three tables have composition relationships with the database, which means that if the database ceases to exist, so do the tables.

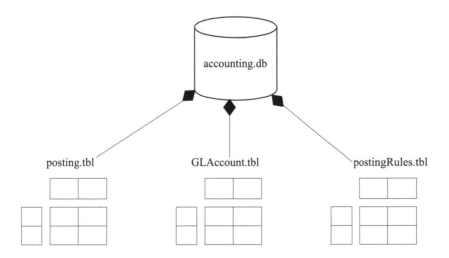

Figure 10-6: Component Diagram with Iconic Stereotypes

Nodes

A **node** is a piece of hardware that represents some kind of computational resource. A node generally has memory; it may have processing capability.

Nodes represent the physical deployment of components across the system's hardware. Another way to look at this is that components "live" on nodes. The nodes that contain deployment components (see Components earlier in this chapter) execute those components.

The UML notation for a node is a cube, as shown in Figure 10-7.

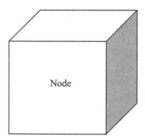

Figure 10-7: Node Notation

Figure 10-8 shows two nodes that form part of our bookstore system. The cube on the right shows an optional way of indicating which components live on a particular node. We'll see some user-defined stereotype icons for nodes in the next section.

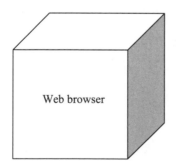 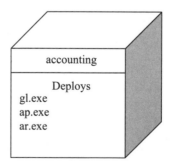

Figure 10-8: Sample Nodes

Deployment Diagrams

A **deployment diagram** shows a collection of nodes, and also the dependencies and associations among those nodes.

On a deployment diagram, an association between nodes represents a physical connection. It's common to see these connections labeled with various user-defined stereotypes, such as «RS-232» and «Ethernet», that indicate the nature of the connections.

Figure 10-9 shows a deployment diagram for The Internet Bookstore. This diagram shows that this set of physical elements of the bookstore system uses a variation of the standard client/server approach, with the various instances of the Web browser representing the client. In this case, the user-defined icons clearly add visual appeal and aid in understanding the diagram.

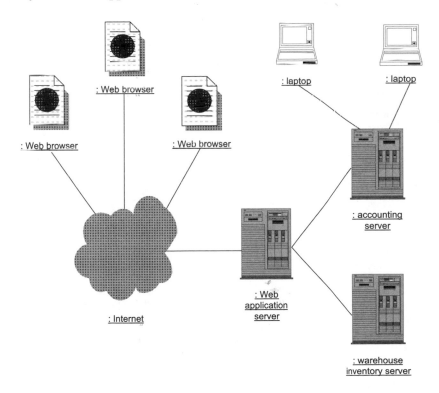

Figure 10-9: Deployment Diagram

The UML also offers a way to show, on a component diagram, the node on which a component lives. You do this using the built-in *location* tagged value. For instance, you might attach the tagged value {location = Accounting-Server} to the GLAccount component introduced in Figure 10-4. This comes in handy when your deployment diagrams use icons rather than the regular cubes to illustrate nodes.

Physical Diagrams and Packages

This section borrows a term from *UML Distilled*: **physical diagrams**, which include component diagrams and deployment diagrams.

The contents of the Unified Process implementation model (see Chapter 2) include component diagrams. Figure 10-10 shows some of the contents of an implementation package for our bookstore.

Naturally, the primary contents of the Unified Process deployment model (see Chapter 2) are deployment diagrams. Figure 10-11 shows some of the contents of a deployment package for our bookstore.

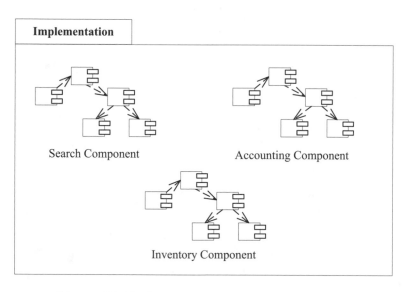

Figure 10-10: Sample Implementation Package

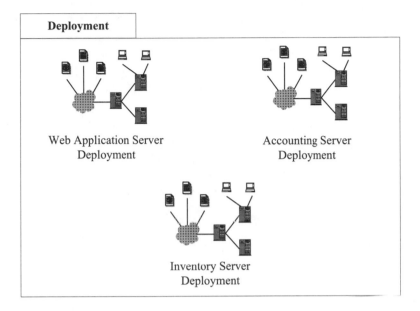

Figure 10-11: Sample Deployment Package

This concludes our tour of the Unified Modeling Language. I hope you enjoyed it.

Glossary

abstract class A *class* that cannot have any *instance*s.

action An executable statement that result in changes in the values of one or more *attribute*s of an *object* or the return of some value(s) to the object that sent a *message*, or both.

active class A *class* whose *instance*s are *active object*s.

active object An *object* that can own a *process* or a *thread*.

activity Something that an *object* performs on an ongoing basis. An activity is nonatomic, which means it can be interrupted.

activity diagram A diagram that shows the flows among *activities* associated with a given *object*, including *transition*s, *branch*es and *merge*s, and *fork*s and *join*s.

actor A role that a user can play with regard to a system; or an entity, such as another system or a database, that resides outside the system.

adornment A piece of information that a modeler can add to enhance a *model* or a piece of a model.

aggregation A "whole/part" relationship within which one or more smaller *class*es are "parts" of a larger "whole" class.

alternate course of action A path through a *use case* that represents an error condition or a path that the *actor* and the system take less frequently. Synonym: *exceptional flow of events*.

analysis class A stereotyped *class* that is represented on one or more *robustness diagram*s.

analysis model A *model* that helps the developers refine and structure the functional requirements captured within the *use case model*. This model contains realizations of *use case*s that lend themselves better than the use cases for design and implementation work.

Analysis workflow Within the Unified Process, the set of activities aimed at building the *analysis model*.

architectural baseline The version of the *architecture* that contains expanded versions of the six models initialized during the *Inception phase*.

architecture The fundamental organization of the system as a whole. Aspects of an architecture include static elements, dynamic elements, how those elements work together, and the overall architectural style that guides the organization of the system. Architecture also addresses issues such as performance, scalability, reuse, and economic and technological constraints.

association A structural connection between *class*es.

association class A cross between an *association* and a *class*, generally used to model an association that has interesting characteristics of its own outside the classes it connects.

attribute A property that describes an *object* or a *class*.

balking message A synchronous *message* that the sending *object* gives up on if the receiving object is not ready to accept it.

basic course of action The sunny-day scenario of a *use case*, the main start-to-finish path that the *actor* and the system will follow under normal circumstances. Synonym: *main flow of events*.

boundary class An *analysis class* to which one or more *boundary object*s belong.

boundary object An object with which an *actor* associated with a *use case* interacts.

branch A decision point, on an *activity diagram*, at which there are two or more possible paths of flow of control.

call action An invocation of a *method* on an *object*.

call event A synchronous communication that involves an *object* invoking a *method* on another object or an object invoking one of its own methods on itself.

candidate architecture An *architecture* made up of initial versions of the *use case model*, the *analysis model*, the *design model*, the *deployment model*, the *implementation model*, and the *test model*.

change event An *event* that occurs when some condition is satisfied.

child The more specific *class* within a *generalization*. Synonym: *subclass*.

class A collection of *object*s that have the same characteristics.

class diagram A diagram that shows *class*es and the various relationships in which they are involved.

collaboration A collection of *class*es, *interface*s, and other elements that work together to provide some behavior.

collaboration diagram A diagram that focuses on the organization of the *object*s that participate in a given set of *message*s.

component A physical and replaceable part of a system that conforms to, and realizes, a set of *interface*s.

component diagram A diagram that shows a collection of related *component*s.

composite state A *state* that can have *substate*s.

composition A strong form of *aggregation* within which the "parts" live and die with the "whole."

concurrent substate A *substate* in which an *object* can reside while also residing in the given *composite state*. The object can be in more than one of the composite state's concurrent substates at a time.

constraint A thing that extends the semantics of an element of a *model* by specifying a condition that must hold true for that element.

Construction phase Within the Unified Process, the *phase* during which the development team tries to build a system that is capable of operating successfully in beta customer environments.

control class An *analysis class* to which one or more *control object*s belong.

control object An *object* that embodies application logic, in the context of robustness analysis.

create action An *action* that results in the creation of an *object*.

cycle A period of time within a development project that ends with the release of a version of the system to customers.

deferred event An event of interest to an *object*, but which the object defers handling until the object reaches a different *state*.

dependency A "using" relationship within which a change in one thing (such as a *class*) may affect another thing (for instance, another class).

deployment component A *component* that represents an executable part of a system.

deployment diagram A diagram that shows a collection of *node*s, and also the *dependencies* and *associations* among those nodes.

deployment model A *model* that defines the physical organization of the system in terms of computational *node*s.

deployment view A view that focuses on the geographic distribution of the various software elements on hardware and the other physical elements that constitute the system.

design class A stereotyped *class* that is represented on one or more design-level *class diagrams*.

design model A *model* that describes the physical realizations of the *use cases*, from the *use case model*, and also the contents of the *analysis model*. The design model serves as an abstraction of the *implementation model*.

design pattern A *pattern* that comes into play during the design phase of a software development project.

design view A *view* that focuses on the things that form the vocabulary of the problem that the system is trying to solve and the elements of the solution to that problem.

Design workflow Within the Unified Process, the set of activities aimed at building the *design model*.

destroy action An *action* that results in the destruction of an *object*.

domain model The set of *class*es that come out of the early stages of a development project.

Elaboration phase Within the Unified Process, the *phase* during which the development team tries to establish the ability to build the new system given the financial constraints, schedule constraints, and other kinds of constraints that the development project faces.

encapsulation The principle under which an *object* hides its data from the rest of the world and only lets outsiders manipulate that data by way of calls to the object's *method*s.

entity class An *analysis class* to which one or more *entity object*s belong.

entity object An *object* that contains long-lived information, such as that associated with databases, in the context of robustness analysis.

entry action An *action* that an *object* always performs immediately upon entering a given *state*.

event An occurrence of interest to an *object*.

exceptional flow of events A path through a *use case* that represents an error condition or a path that the *actor* and the system take less frequently. Synonym: *alternate course of action*.

execution component A *component* that's created as a result of an executing system.

exit action An *action* that an *object* always performs immediately before leaving a given *state*, in response to a regular *transition* or a *self-transition*.

extend A relationship within which a base *use case* implicitly includes the behavior of another use case at one or more specified *extension point*s.

extension point A point in a *use case* from which an *extend* relationship goes out to another use case.

final state The stopping point for the *state machine* for an *object*.

focus of control A tall, thin rectangle that sits on top of an *object*'s *lifeline* on a *sequence diagram*.

fork A splitting of a flow of control on an *activity diagram* into two or more flows of control, each of which operates independent of, and concurrent with, the others.

forward engineering The process of generating code from *model*s.

framework An architectural *pattern* that provides a template that one can use to extend applications.

generalization A relationship between a general class (the *superclass* or *parent*) and a more specific version of that class (the *subclass* or *child*).

You can think of the subclass as being a kind of the superclass. Generalization also applies to *use cases*.

guard condition. A Boolean expression that must evaluate to True in order for a *branch* on an *activity diagram* to be taken, or for a *transition* on a *statechart diagram* to fire.

history state A special *state* that "remembers" the last *substate* that an *object* is in when that object leaves the given *composite state*.

implementation model A *model* that describes how the elements of the *design model* have been packaged into software *components*, such as source code files, dynamic link libraries (DLLs), and Enterprise Java Beans (EJBs).

implementation view A *view* that focuses on the things that the project team assembles to form the physical system.

Implementation workflow Within the Unified Process, the set of activities aimed at building the *implementation model*.

Inception phase Within the Unified Process, the *phase* during which the development team tries to establish the case for the viability of the proposed system.

include A relationship within which one *use case* explicitly includes the behavior of another use case at a specified point within a *basic course of action* or an *alternate course of action*.

increment A release of the system that contains added or improved functionality over and above the previous release.

inheritance The feature of object orientation by which a *class* receives attributes and operations from a parent class.

Initial Operational Capability The *major milestone* associated with the *Construction phase*.

initial state The starting point of the *state machine* for an *object*.

instance With regard to a *class*, an *object* that belongs to that class.

interaction diagram A diagram that shows how a set of *objects* interact with each other. There are two kinds of interaction diagrams: *collaboration diagrams* and *sequence diagrams*.

interface A collection of *operation*s that represents services offered by a *class* or a *component*.

internal transition An *action* that an *object* performs in response to the reception of an *event* while remaining in its current *state*.

iteration A mini-project that is part of a *workflow*.

join A synchronization of two or more flows of control on an *activity diagram* into one flow.

Life-Cycle Architecture The *major milestone* associated with the *Elaboration phase*.

Life-Cycle Objectives The *major milestone* associated with the *Inception phase*.

lifeline A dashed line on a *sequence diagram* that represents the life, and perhaps the death, of an *object*.

main flow of events The sunny-day scenario of a *use case*, the main start-to-finish path that the *actor* and the system will follow under normal circumstances. Synonym: *basic course of action*.

major milestone A point at which managers make important decisions about whether to proceed with development, and, if so, what's required.

mechanism A *design pattern* that applies to a society of *class*es.

merge A point on an *activity diagram* at which two or more *branch*ed paths come together.

message A communication between two *object*s, or within an object, that is designed to result in some activity.

method A function that uses or changes the values of one or more of an *object*'s *attribute*s.

model A simplification of reality that helps people understand the complexity inherent in software.

multiple inheritance *Inheritance* that involves more than one parent *class*.

multiplicity A value that indicates how many *object*s associated with a given *class* can be present within a particular *association*.

N-ary association A relationship that involves three or more *class*es.

node A piece of hardware that represents some kind of computational resource. A node generally has memory; it may have processing capability.

note An *adornment* that records a comment without having any effect on the *model* within which it appears.

object A real-world thing or concept.

object diagram A snapshot of part of the structure of the system being modeled. It has the same basic appearance as a *class diagram*, except that it shows *object*s, and actual values for *attribute*s, instead of *class*es.

object flow A *dependency* that shows the details of how *object*s involved in the various *activities* and *action*s shown on an *activity diagram* are specifically affected.

operation A service, defined for a *class*, that an *object* can request to affect behavior.

package A conceptual grouping of pieces of a *model*.

parameterized collaboration A *collaboration* that acts like a *template class*, but has *role*s as its formal parameters, instead of *attribute*s or data types.

parent The more general *class* within a *generalization*. Synonym: *superclass*.

path name An extended form of the name of an element of a *model* that describes the *package* that includes the element.

pattern A solution to a problem that's common to a variety of contexts.

phase The span of time between two *major milestone*s. The Unified Process defines four phases: the *Inception phase*, the *Elaboration phase*, the *Construction phase*, and the *Transition phase*.

physical diagram A diagram that shows a set of physical elements of a system. There are two kinds of physical diagrams: *component diagram*s and *deployment diagram*s.

polymorphism A principle of object orientation that states that an *object* of a *subclass* can redefine any of the *operation*s it *inherits* from its *superclass*(es).

private visibility The *visibility* value that specifies that only *object*s belonging to a given *class* can use a particular *attribute* or *operation*.

process A heavyweight flow of control. Generally, a program running under an operating system such as Windows or UNIX lives within a process, and each process has some kind of unique identifier.

process view A *view* that focuses on those aspects of the system that involve timing and the flow of control.

Product Release The *major milestone* associated with the *Transition phase*.

protected visibility The *visibility* value that specifies that only *object*s that belong to *subclass*es of a particular *class* (at any level below that class) can use a given *attribute* or *operation*.

public visibility The *visibility* value that specifies that *object*s of any *class* can use a given *attribute* or *operation*.

realization The relationship between an *interface* and a *class* or *component* that provides the interface's *operation*s, or between a *use case* and the *collaboration* that represents the implementation of that use case.

realize To provide a *realization*, that is, a concrete representation of an abstract concept.

Requirements workflow Within the Unified Process, the set of activities aimed at building the *use case model*.

responsibility With regard to a *class*, the obligations that the class has with respect to other classes.

return action The return of a value in response to a *call action*.

reverse engineering The construction (or reconstruction) of *model*s from code.

robustness analysis The process of analyzing the text of a *use case* and identifying a first-guess set of *object*s that will participate in the use case, and then classifying these objects based on their characteristics.

robustness diagram A diagram that shows *object*s that belong to *analysis class*es, and the relationships among those objects, in connection with a *use case*.

role A face that a *class* presents to other classes within an *association* or a *parameterized collaboration*.

round-trip engineering The combination of *forward engineering* and *reverse engineering*.

self-transition A *transition* whose *source state* and *target state* are the same.

send action An *action* that sends a *signal* to an *object*.

sequence diagram A diagram that focuses on the time ordering of *messages* that go back and forth between *object*s.

sequential substate A *substate* in which an *object* can reside while also residing in the given *composite state*. The object can be in only one of the composite state's sequential substates at a time.

signal An asynchronous communication between *object*s: one object "throws" a signal to another object that "catches" the signal; the sender of the signal doesn't expect a response from the receiver.

single inheritance *Inheritance* that involves only one parent *class*.

source state The "from" *state* within a *transition* between states.

state A condition in which an *object* can be at some point during its lifetime, for some finite amount of time.

statechart diagram A diagram that shows an *object*'s *state machine*.

state diagram See *statechart diagram*.

state machine The combination of the *state*s that an *object* can assume during its life, the *event*s to which that object can respond, the possible responses the object can make to those events, and the *transition*s that occur between the object's states.

stereotype A thing that extends the basic vocabulary of the UML.

subclass The more specific *class* within a *generalization*. Synonym: *child*.

substate A state within a *composite state*.

substitutability A principle of object orientation that states that an *object* of a *subclass* may be substituted anywhere an object of an associated *superclass* is used.

subsystem A *stereotype*d *package* that groups related elements to form part of a *system*.

superclass The more general *class* within a *generalization*. Synonym: *parent*.

swimlane A lane on an *activity diagram* down which one can track *activities* and *action*s associated with, for instance, a particular part of an organization.

synchronization bar A long, thin black rectangle that represents either a *fork* or a *join* on an *activity diagram*.

system A *stereotype*d *package* that contains all of the *model*s that a development team has produced.

tagged value A thing that extends the properties of a *model* element, but not *instance*s of that element.

target state The "to" *state* within a *transition* between states.

template class A construct that represents a family of potential *class*es. A template class has a set of formal parameters; a modeler uses the template to create a new class by binding a set of actual parameters to the template.

test model A *model* that describes how integration and system tests will exercise executable *component*s from the *implementation model*.

Test workflow Within the Unified Process, the set of activities aimed at building the *test model*.

thread A lightweight flow of control that generally runs inside a *process*.

time event An *event* that occurs after a specified period of time.

time expression An expression that resolves to a relative or absolute value of time once it's evaluated.

timeout message A synchronous *message* for which the sending *object* waits only for a specified period for the receiver to get ready to accept the message.

timing constraint A condition that must be satisfied with regard to time. A timing constraint usually contains a *time expression*; it may also contain a *timing mark*.

timing mark A time-related name or label on a *message*.

transition A path between *activities* on an *activity diagram*, or between *state*s on a *statechart diagram*.

Transition phase Within the Unified Process, the *phase* during which the development team tries to roll out the fully functional system to its customers.

triggerless transition A *transition* that fires unconditionally when an *object* is ready to move from one *state* to another, or a transition between one *activity* or *action* and another activity or action on an *activity diagram*.

use case A sequence of actions that an *actor* performs within a system to achieve a particular goal.

use case diagram A diagram that shows *actors* and *use case*s and the relationships among them.

use case model A *model* that captures the functional requirements of the system. This model allows the project stakeholders to agree on the capabilities of the system and the conditions to which it must conform.

use case realization—analysis A *collaboration* that describes how a *use case* is *realize*d and performed in terms of *analysis object*s.

use case view A *view* that focuses on the scenarios executed by human users and also external systems.

view A particular set of aspects of the system as seen from a given perspective, which in effect hides other aspects that are not of concern to the viewer.

visibility The property of an *attribute* or an *operation*, belonging to a class, that specifies whether *object*s that belong to other *class*es can "see" that attribute or operation.

workflow Within the Unified Process, a set of activities that various project workers perform. The Unified Process defines five core workflows: the *Requirements workflow*, the *Analysis workflow*, the *Design workflow*, the *Implementation workflow*, and the *Test workflow*.

work product component A *component* that's part of the system but isn't executable.

INDEX ▼ 143

Index

A

abstract class
  defined 75
  example 76
  notation 76
action
  defined 59, 89
  examples 64, 90, 103
  notation 60, 61, 62, 63, 90
active class
  defined 96
  example 97
  notation 97
active object
  defined 96
  example 97
  notation 97
activity
  defined 89
  examples 90
  notation 90
activity diagram
  defined 94
  example 95
actor
  defined 39
  examples 40
  notation 40
addOnly property 79
adornments
  and classes 26
  notes 35
aggregation
  defined 27
  examples 30
  notation 29, 30

alternate course of action
  defined 43
  examples 44, 46
analysis class
  and packages 72
  types 53
analysis model
  analysis classes 53
  Analysis workflow 15
  and architecture 15
  defined 14
  packages of classes 37
  robustness diagrams 72
  and use case model 13
  use cases 49
analysis package 72, 73
Analysis workflow
  activities 14
  and frameworks 117
  robustness analysis 53
  and Unified Process phases 15
architectural baseline 11, 19
architecture 7
architecture-centric 11
association
  defined 25
  examples 26, 27, 28
  name 26, 27
  navigation 27
  notation 26
association class
  defined 30
  example 33
  notation 32

From the Addison-Wesley Object Technology Series
Series Editors: Grady Booch, James Rumbaugh, Ivar Jacobson

UML Distilled, Second Edition
A Brief Guide to the Standard Object Modeling Language
Martin Fowler and Kendall Scott

The award-winning first edition of *UML Distilled* was widely praised for being a concise guide to the core parts of the UML and has proved extremely successful in helping developers get up and running quickly. *UML Distilled, Second Edition* maintains the concise format with significantly updated coverage of use cases and activity diagrams and expanded coverage of collaborations. It also includes a new appendix detailing the changes between UML versions.

0-201-65783-X • Paperback • 224 pages • ©2000

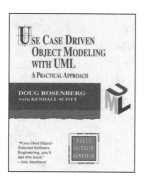

Use Case Driven Object Modeling with UML
A Practical Approach
Doug Rosenberg and Kendall Scott

Use Case Driven Object Modeling with UML provides practical guidance that shows developers how to produce UML models with a minimal startup time, while maintaining traceability from user requirements through detailed designing and coding. The authors present proven methods for driving the object modeling process forward in a straightforward manner.

0-201-43289-7 • Paperback • 192 pages • ©1999

Developing Applications with Visual Basic and UML
Paul R. Reed Jr.

Developing Applications with Visual Basic and UML describes a proven development process for designing and implementing object-oriented client/server applications in VB using the Unified Modeling Language (UML). Through a significant case study, the author demonstrates the design benefits of UML and shows how to translate a UML specification into Visual Basic code.

0-201-61579-7 • Paperback • 592 pages • ©2000

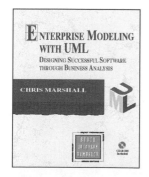

Enterprise Modeling with UML
Designing Successful Software through Business Analysis
Chris Marshall

Written for practitioners interested in business systems and software applications, *Enterprise Modeling with UML* fuses object technology, workflow, data warehousing, and distributed system concepts into a coherent model that has been successfully implemented worldwide. This book describes specific methods for modeling large, complex, and adaptable enterprise systems, using the Unified Modeling Language (UML) to illustrate its concepts and components.

0-201-43313-3 • Paperback w/CD-ROM • 288 pages • ©2000

Building Web Applications with UML
Jim Conallen

Building Web Applications with UML is a guide to building robust, scalable, and feature-rich Web applications using proven object-oriented techniques. Written for the project manager, architect, analyst, designer, and programmer of Web applications, this book examines the unique aspects of modeling Web applications with the Web Application Extension (WAE) for the Unified Modeling Language (UML).

0-201-61577-0 • Paperback • 320 pages • ©2000

Fundamentals of Object-Oriented Design in UML
Meilir Page-Jones

With the Unified Modeling Language (UML), programmers are equipped with a powerful tool for expressing software designs. *Fundamentals of Object-Oriented Design in UML* shows aspiring and experienced programmers alike how to apply design concepts, the UML, and the best practices in OO development to improve both their code and their success rates with object-based projects.

0-201-69946-X • Paperback • 480 pages • ©2000

Real-Time UML, Second Edition
Developing Efficient Objects for Embedded Systems
Bruce Powel Douglass

Real-Time UML, Second Edition, provides an overview of the essentials of real-time systems and an introduction to UML that focuses on its use in design and development. The book examines requirements analysis, the definition of object structure and object behavior, architectural design, mechanistic design, and more detailed designs that encompass data structure, operations, and exceptions.

0-201-65784-8 • Paperback • 368 pages • ©2000

The Unified Modeling Language User Guide
Grady Booch, James Rumbaugh, and Ivar Jacobson

In *The Unified Modeling Language User Guide*, the original developers of the UML—Grady Booch, James Rumbaugh, and Ivar Jacobson—provide a tutorial to the core aspects of the language in a two-color format designed to facilitate learning. Starting with a conceptual model of the UML, the book progressively applies the UML to a series of increasingly complex modeling problems across a variety of application domains.

0-201-57168-4 • Hardcover • 512 pages • ©1999

The Unified Modeling Language Reference Manual
James Rumbaugh, Ivar Jacobson, and Grady Booch

The Unified Modeling Language (UML) has rapidly become the standard notation for modeling software-intensive systems. This book provides the definitive description of UML from its original developers. Whether you are capturing requirements, developing a software architecture, designing the implementation, or trying to understand an existing system, this is the book for you.

0-201-30998-X • Herdcover w/CD-ROM • 576 pages • ©1999

The Unified Software Development Process
Ivar Jacobson, Grady Booch, and James Rumbaugh

This landmark book provides a thorough overview of the Unified Process for software development, with a practical focus on modeling using the Unified Modeling Language (UML). The Unified Process goes beyond mere object-oriented analysis and design to spell out a proven family of techniques that supports the complete software development life cycle. The result is a component-based process that is use-case driven, architecture-centric, iterative, and incremental.

0-201-57169-2 • Hardcover • 512 pages • ©1999

From the Addison-Wesley Software Components Series
Series Editor: Clemens Szyperski

UML Components
A Simple Process for Specifying Component-Based Software
John Cheesman and John Daniels

UML Components applies UML to the world of component architecture, demonstrating how it can be used to specify components, their interactions, and their integration into cohesive systems. This book shows readers which elements of UML apply to server-side component-based development and how to use them most effectively. The authors walk through requirements definition, component identification, component interaction, component specification, and provisioning and assembly.

0-201-70851-5 • Paperback • 208 pages • ©2001

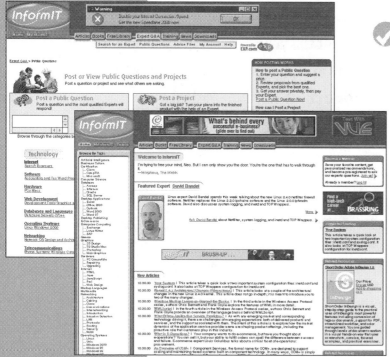

Register
Your Book

at www.aw.com/cseng/register

You may be eligible to receive:

- Advance notice of forthcoming editions of the book
- Related book recommendations
- Chapter excerpts and supplements of forthcoming titles
- Information about special contests and
  promotions throughout the year
- Notices and reminders about author appearances,
  tradeshows, and online chats with special guests

Contact us

If you are interested in writing a book or reviewing
manuscripts prior to publication, please write to us at:

Editorial Department
Addison-Wesley Professional
75 Arlington Street, Suite 300
Boston, MA 02116 USA
Email: AWPro@aw.com

Addison-Wesley

Visit us on the Web: http://www.aw.com/cseng